STRANGE GODS

STRANGE GODS

Contemporary Religious Cults in America

William J. Whalen

OUR SUNDAY VISITOR, INC., Publisher

HUNTINGTON, INDIANA

Library of Congress Catalog Card No. 80-81451
ISBN 0-87973-666-6

OUR SUNDAY VISITOR, INC.
200 NOLL PLAZA
HUNTINGTON, INDIANA 46750

PRINTED IN U.S.A.

81 82 83 84 85 10 9 8 7 6 5 4 3 2 1

Contents

Preface

No one can ignore the growth of cults and Eastern religions in the United States in recent years. Their activities make headlines; their missionary tactics have become topics for TV talk-shows and newspaper columnists; their leaders have become better known than the heads of most Protestant denominations.

This book seeks to examine some of the religious cults that have achieved national prominence in the United States. No single book can begin to catalog the hundreds of minor cults that have sprung up since the 1960s. Some of these groups certainly reflect distinctive religious doctrines and lifestyles but are unknown outside their own neighborhood or city. Readers interested in local cults not discussed in this book may find information in some of the books listed in the general bibliography.

I write from the perspective of a Roman Catholic who has observed and written about American religious groups for 30 years. My co-religionists might consider that 25 to 35 percent of the members of some of the more widely publicized cults have come from Roman Catholic backgrounds. The Pied Pipers of the cults have attracted others besides refugees from the counterculture and young people from broken homes. Thousands of the cults' devotees once attended Mass in their parish churches, went to parochial schools, and enjoyed the security of loving families.

This book focuses on *contemporary* religious cults, those which have been founded, or which experienced their greatest growth, during the second half of the 20th century. Some of these cults (such as astrology and witchcraft) represent ancient beliefs that have enjoyed a remarkable revival in our day.

I have tried to be objective in describing what these cults believe, how they worship, how they seek funds and converts, what lifestyles they impose, and so on. Unlike a number of evangelical Protestant students of the cults, I have not sought to present a proof-text refutation of cult doctrines. Neither have I hesitated to rattle some of the skeletons in the cultic closets even though doing so may displease the publicists for the various cults.

I would like to thank the editors of *U.S. Catholic* and Claretian Publications for allowing me to include in these chapters material that originally appeared in their publications.

W.J.W.

Lafayette, Indiana
January 1981

STRANGE GODS

CHAPTER I

The World of Cults

*Millions in the U.S. give allegiance
to old myths and new messiahs.*

Small numbers of Americans have always preferred the religious milieu of the
cults to that of the mainline churches. They have joined the Shakers or the Spiritualists or the Swedenborgians rather than the Baptists or Methodists. Consequently their neighbors may have viewed them as somewhat strange, but with a
few exceptions they have been free to believe and practice their faiths without
harassment.

While 19th-century cultists numbered in the thousands, today's cults report a
combined membership in the millions. The growth of these cults, their fund-
raising techniques, their impact on family life, and their proselytism have
fascinated the average American, as well as students of comparative religion.

Parents, clergymen, and lawyers debate the wisdom and legality of "deprogramming" members of the Children of God, the Unification Church, and other cults. Air travelers find it difficult to avoid the ubiquitous Hare Kirshna devotee who tries to foist booklets on them as they try to make plane connections. A
federal court convicts nine top Scientologists on charges of conspiring to steal
government documents. Two members of Synanon, a drug-rehabilitation program that evolved into a cult, were charged with putting a rattlesnake in the
mailbox of an attorney who had won a $300,000 judgment against the group.

Reports of such cult activity helped spice the nightly TV-network news and
enliven front pages. Many Americans have looked on the world of the cults with
an amused tolerance. The parents, relatives, and friends of young cultists are

more likely to view the cult scene with despair and fear. But the nation was stunned in November 1978 when Congressman Leo Ryan and three newspeople were murdered by members of a cult most people had never heard of. They would barely comprehend the subsequent deaths, by murder and suicide, of more than 900 members of the Peoples Temple cult at Jonestown, Guyana, at the bidding of their leader, Rev. Jim Jones.

Citizens began calling for a federal investigation of the cults. Some demanded new laws to restrict cult activity. Were some of these cults engaged in brainwashing their teen-age converts? Did the prophet-founders and top officials of some of these groups enrich themselves by camouflaging a money-making scheme as a religion? Did the fund-raising methods of some cults come under the heading of charity fraud?

The federal government has always hesitated to interject itself into religious questions. Only in rare situations have state or federal authorities ventured into this delicate area. The federal government did reject the claims of the 19th-century Mormons that polygamy was a religious practice protected by the First Amendment. States have told cultic snake-handlers that their ritual violates the law. Government officials take a dim view of cults that insist that the ritual-use of marijuana or other drugs qualifies as a sacrament. The state occasionally directs that a child receive a blood transfusion despite the objections of the Jehovah's Witnesses parents.

But except for these special cases, the U.S. government keeps hands off religious beliefs and practices. In a pluralistic society such as that of the U.S., the state claims no competence to judge the truth or falsity of religious dogma. In effect, the state protects the right of anyone to believe what he or she wishes and to contribute time and money to any cause. This includes the right to be duped and the right to give money to a charlatan.

Despite the Jonestown tragedy, thoughtful people will think twice before inviting the federal government to intervene in the realm of religion. Anyone with $5 to spare can receive a mail-order ordination as a minister, and any con-man can set up a new church. But such may be the price we Americans pay for our freedom of religion. Unless a cult violates the law by kidnapping "converts," abusing its tax-exempt status, threatening or murdering critics, or otherwise breaking the laws of the land, it receives the same First Amendment protection as any mainline church.

While many of the cults we will examine simply provide alternative belief systems, a few display all the characteristics of another Peoples Temple and their leaders show themselves to be as unstable and paranoid as the Rev. Jim Jones. If the government is not the appropriate agency to identify these cults, citizens must turn to the press to get their information. Cults that demand protection because the Constitution guarantees freedom of religion cannot deny others the right to examine their beliefs and practices in a free press. Some cults with enormous financial assets at their disposal, helped by batteries of lawyers, try to suppress all criticism by filing (or threatening to file) libel suits. They seldom win any of these suits, but they know the threat of litigation can intimidate writers and publications lacking the funds to defend themselves in court actions.

The tragedy at Jonestown might have been prevented if the press had not ignored the suicide rituals at the Peoples Temple and the megalomania of the cult's leader. Few of the cults we will be looking at have broken the law, and fewer have the potential of another Jonestown; but no cult can claim immunity from investigation by responsible journalists.

In approaching the question of the cults, the first problem we encounter is: What constitutes a cult? Scholars give differing answers, although most of us would recognize the difference between, say, the Presbyterian Church and the Hare Krishna movement.

One evangelical Protestant writer, David Breese, calls a cult "a religious perversion. It is a belief and practice in the world of religion which calls for devotion to a religious view or leader centered on false doctrine. It is an organized heresy." Probably no sociologist or student of comparative religion would be comfortable with this definition.

Some evangelicals seem to extend the term "cult" to any group that differs from their understanding of Christianity. They disagree about whether the Seventh-day Adventist Church is a cult or just a Protestant church with some unusual views. A well known critic of the cults, Walter Martin, considers even the Unitarian Church a cult.

Prof. Robert S. Ellwood, Jr., of the University of Southern California defines a cult as involving a search for an ecstatic state: "A cult is a group derived from the experience of one or a few individuals who are able to enter (or are fascinated by the possibility of entering) a superior, ecstatic state of consciousness in which contact and rapport with all reaches of a non-historical and impersonal universe are possible with the help of intermediaries (human and/or supernatural)" (*Religious and Spiritual Groups in Modern America*, p. 19). This definition would seem to exclude such cults as the Jehovah's Witnesses, who spend hundreds of hours a year trudging door-to-door but never consider that the founder of the faith or his successors experienced a "superior, ecstatic state."

Other scholars suggest that a cult forms around a living founder-prophet and somehow ceases to be a cult when the founder dies. This approach presents problems of its own. Excactly how does a cult change the day after the founder dies?

Journalist Tom Wolfe offered a succinct definition in the December 1979 issue of *Esquire:* "A cult is a religion with no political power." In my view, the most useful definition is that formulated by Charles Braden about 30 years ago: "A cult is any religious group which differs significantly in some one or more respects as to belief or practices from those religious groups which are regarded as the normative expressions of religion in our total culture" *(These Also Believe,* p. xii).

Applying this latter definition, one finds it understandable that early Christianity was seen as a Judaic cult by the ancient Romans, just as Buddhism arose as a cult derived from Hinduism. Even today a Christian denomination might be viewed as a cult by the people of a predominantly Muslim or atheist country.

Unfortunately the term "cult" is often applied and understood in a pejorative sense. No one stands up and brags, "I belong to a cult." Rather than "cult," some writers prefer to use the expression "minority religion." But the media and the general public are not likely to give up the use of "cult" to label certain religious groups. For whereas all cults *are* minority religious groups, not all minority religious groups (such as the Salvation Army or Quakers or Mennonites) are properly described as cults.

Although several million Americans belong to the hundreds of contemporary cults, recent publicity surrounding the cult movement has perhaps tended to inflate the numerical strength of these groups. In a letter soliciting a $60 annual membership in the Cult and Occult Unification Program (COUP), Walter Martin maintains: "Recent statistics reveal that 84,000,000 Americans are lost in the cult-occult movements now. This represents 39% of the total population" (dated Feb. 14, 1977). This may be the highest estimate of cult affiliation anyone has yet suggested.

Scores of cults remain unknown to all but their devotees and people in the neighborhood. Their founders never are mentioned in the national media. On the other hand, the high visibility of a band of bald, saffron-robed Hare Krishna cultists may lead the average person to imagine that their numbers far exceed the several thousand U.S. devotees. The total U.S. membership of the Hare Krishnas, Moonies, and Children of God in 1980 is fewer than 20,000.

Some of the inflated totals of cult membership may be explained by the habit of some reporters of taking the membership claims of certain cults at face value. Common sense tells us that the Church of Scientology, for example, has nowhere near the 5,437,000 members claimed worldwide in its fewer than 255 churches and missions; yet this figure has been repeated in several national magazines.

Cults are flourishing and taking up the religious slack in the U.S., as most mainline denominations decline, according to the report of a team of sociologists from the University of Washington. They found a correlation between low church-membership in a state and the popularity of the cults. In their study, presented at the 1980 meeting of the American Association for the Advancement of Science, they listed the top ten "cult states" according to the ratio of cult members to the general population. The states are Nevada, New Mexico, California, Colorado, Arizona, Oregon, Hawaii, New York, Missouri, and Illinois. California alone has been identified as headquarters for more than 150 groups classified as religious cults. The University of Washington sociologists found a "cult belt" extending along the West coast from Southern California to Alaska. "Cults will continue to proliferate as secularization makes ruins of the dominant churches, and in time some of these cults may become dominant religions," they predicted.

Cults come and go. No one has devised a foolproof method to predict the survival of a particular cult. Some groups once active on the American scene have simply disappeared: Father Divine's Peace Mission, Psychiana, Shakerism. Others, such as the I Am movement, have shrunk to insignificance. A hundred or so years ago, someone might have predicted that Mormonism would collapse after the murder of its founder; but the Church of Jesus Christ of Latter-day Saints (Mormons) is thriving and counts more than 2,500,000 U.S. members out of a world total of 4,000,000.

The degree of involvement and commitment varies greatly from cult to cult and from individual to individual. The tabloid readers who check their horoscope every day out of curiosity stand at one end of the cult spectrum; the dedicated members of a Children of God colony or Moonie commune stand at the other. Some extremist cults demand total commitment, communal living, and absolute obedience to a charismatic leader; other cults even tolerate their members' affiliation with another church.

The potential for psychic damage also varies from one group to another. Some of the groups we will examine are led by people at least as paranoid as Jim Jones apparently was. Other cults simply attract men and women looking for community, self-improvement, kicks, esoteric knowledge, tranquillity, a father-figure, or an answer to the meaning of existence.

For most cults, the target group for recruiting is that of white middle-class men and women in their late teens or early 20s. To avoid possible legal problems, the cults usually steer clear of young people under 18. Unlike the Mormons and Jehovah's Witnesses, who concentrate on door-to-door missionary work, most of the newer cults show little interest in middle-aged prospects. (In several respects, the Peoples Temple differed from most of the cults that have made the headlines. It was actually a *congregation* in good standing of the 1,278,000-member Disciples of Christ denomination, and it drew most of its adherents from the ranks of lower-income blacks.)

By zeroing in on the 18- to 25-year-olds, the contemporary cults reach many people who may be lonely, may be facing a difficult career choice, or may be encountering conflicting moral values for the first time. A visit to a college dormitory on a Friday night when most students are away partying may turn up likely prospects for cult membership. For thousands of young people, a cult may appear to offer an escape from the hard transition between adolescent and adult life. They accept the father-figure in the person of the cult's prophet, who then "frees" them from having to make major decisions about their lives.

Rabbi A. James Rudin, a student of cult activities, believes that there is a "systematic campaign to lure young Jews into religious cults." Although Jews account for less than 3 percent of the U.S. population, Rabbi Rudin says that at least 10 percent of the Moonies come from Jewish homes. His studies indicate that a similarly high proportion of Jews have joined such groups as the Scientologists, Hare Krishnas, and The Way. "I can't say I'm surprised by the statistics," he adds. "We all know Jews fit into the prime target for the cults — middle-class to upper-middle-class white kids, away from home at college, searching for something."

The permissive atmosphere of many college campuses repels some young men and women, and they find a sense of security in a cult that outlaws drugs, liquor, raunchy language, and illicit sex. The Moonie, for example, has no money problems, no big decisions, and not even a need to choose a mate: Father Moon matches worthy couples who may be strangers until the day of their engagement ceremony.

Other practices reinforce the cult's hold on its devotees. Some cults practice secret rituals that give participants the feeling they have been privileged beyond ordinary mortals. Groups such as the Children of God and Hare Krishnas adopt a mode of dress that sets members apart from others and thereby fosters a feeling of comradeship in the face of ridicule from outsiders. Also, most of the cults' prophet-founders claim special revelations from God or special insights into the scriptures, which they are willing to share with those who submit to their spiritual direction. Typically a cult encourages group paranoia, which views all outsiders, even parents, as "tools of Satan" or the equivalent.

Extremist cults are characterized by absolute devotion to a living leader, a claim to complete and absolute truth, a theory that the end justifies the means, and a fear of the larger society. These cults usually expect the devotee to turn over all assets on initiation and to continue to turn over whatever he or she earns or begs to the cult officials. The twin objectives of fund-raising and convert-seeking occupy most of the cultists' waking hours.

The devastation that many of these cults have inflicted on families is hard to overestimate. One day a son or daughter is pursuing a college education, and the next thing the parents hear is that their child is selling peanuts or candles and living in a cult commune. A few parents seem to consider any religion better than none, and some see their children's cult affiliation as an alternative to drug addiction or sexual promiscuity. But most fathers and mothers whose children have joined a cult enter a period of guilty feelings, depression, helplessness, despair, anger, and, especially since Jonestown, fear.

Parents and friends should understand that no family can guarantee immunity from the attraction a cult may have for a vulnerable young person. A weekend of psychological manipulation, intense peer pressure, sleep deprivation, and sophisticated brainwashing techniques can weaken the spiritual defenses of many college students who would normally shrug off the preaching of a religious fanatic.

Those who have counseled hundreds of distraught parents urge them: to keep the lines of communication open to their children if at all possible; to avoid direct confrontations and ultimatums; and to assure the sons and daughters that they will be welcome whenever they choose to return home.

People do drift in and out of most of the cults. One day they may look back on the months or years they spent in the cult as simply an unbelievable and weird time of their youth.

Some devotees come to perceive that begging money to keep the cult leaders in a life of luxury is not helping the world to become a better place to live. They see that it is not their cult which is staffing the hospitals and schools or feeding the hungry or giving shelter to the homeless. This recognition of the true nature of their cult may enable them to cut their ties with it and re-enter the world.

For other young cultists, the constant peer pressure, inadequate diet, lack of sleep, isolation, and daily indoctrination reduce them to the state of spiritual zombies. They may even be the victims of hypnotic techniques.

Hundreds of parents have been driven to employ a professional "deprogrammer" who will abduct their sons and daughters, singly, and attempt to persuade them to leave the cult. Groups such as the American Civil Liberties Union oppose all deprogramming efforts but show little interest in investigating the numerous charges of brainwashing by the cults. The ACLU accuses the deprogrammers of making a good living by their activities, but is silent about the lifestyles of a Rev. Moon, L. Ron Hubbard, or Maharaj Ji.

The average American is well advised to keep informed about contemporary religious cults. These cults are a fact of life, and many of them are likely to be around for some years.

CHAPTER II

Witchcraft and the Occult.

*Twentieth-century witches seek to propagate
the old religion.*

In Europe during the Middle Ages, or in New England during the 17th century, anybody who admitted, much less boasted, that he or she was a witch risked a trial and execution. Witches were considered a clear and present danger to the well-being of both State and Church.

Today, TV talk-shows feature witches along with the usual roster of night-club comics, singers, movie stars, athletes, celebrities, and semi-celebrities. A witch is nowadays more likely to be the star attraction at a chic cocktail party than to be regarded as a danger to the community.

Moviegoers thought they were getting a glimpse of modern-day witchcraft in *Rosemary's Baby* (1968), but the movie's mixture of Satanism and witchcraft bore little resemblance to the real thing. Even less authentic was the TV show *Bewitched*, which featured Elizabeth Montgomery as a nose-twitching witch married to an innocent. But witches do practice their craft in the 1980s; and, although certain aspects of the craft remain hidden to all but initiates, we can discover a great deal about the Old Religion — also called Wicca, the Craft of the Wise.

While all occult movements may be classified as cults, not all cults, nor even many of them, strictly speaking belong in the realm of the occult. A cult may teach bizarre doctrines and appeal to special revelations or biblical interpretations; but one of the distinguishing characteristics of an occult group is its claim to possess hidden or secret knowledge. This knowledge, usually attributed to ancient sources, is carefully guarded and imparted to initiates only after a period of instruction, and often during secret rites. This world of the occult is peopled by witches, theosophists, practitioners of magic, Satanists, spiritists, alchemists, and the like.

Books about witchcraft and other "occult arts" have become so numerous that large bookstores reserve special alcoves for their display. One New York store specializing in occult titles reports (1979) sales are up 100 percent in three years. Occult shops operated by witches and neopagans in the larger cities carry a full line of books and occult items. Sarah Morrison's book titled *The Modern Witches' Spellbook* is advertised as being "for those who'd like to be witches and get their hands on a batch of castable spells." This book also includes a shopping guide for such necessities as bottled bat's blood. *Today's Witches*, by Susy Smith, estimates there are about 60,000 active witches in the United States. (A more likely estimate would be a couple of thousand in perhaps 300 "covens" and another few thousand self-appointed solitary witches.)

Fortunately for today's witches, the climate of opinion in the United States has become more tolerant than in an earlier age; in 1692 and 1693 the citizens of Salem, Massachusetts, hanged 19 people found guilty of witchcraft. During the late Middle Ages, the toll of witches burned at the stake in the city of Würzberg, Germany, in one year exceeded 900. The last of the antiwitchcraft laws in England were repealed only in 1951. The British Medical Association says there are some 7,000 witches plying their trade, including arts of healing, in England. They operate mostly in rural areas — or in cities where regular M.D.s are reluctant to make house-calls. In Africa, the witch doctor retains his influence among the unsophisticated.

The best known witch on the contemporary scene, Sybil Leek, came to the U.S. from England, where she said she could trace her witch ancestry back to 1134. She now lives in a Florida mansion, appears on talk shows, and writes books about witchcraft, astrology, spells, and ghosts.

Recently the U.S. armed forces paid $30,000 to a private research firm to prepare a study of witchcraft and Satanism for the use of chaplains who might be called upon to minister to devotees. The study advised that, in case a devotee should be near death, "it would be permissible for any chaplain to offer spiritual comfort." It described three basic kinds of rituals: "sexual rituals, to fulfill a desire; compassionate rituals, to help another; and destructive rituals, used for anger, annoyance, or hate."

Witchcraft claims to be the continuation of the pagan religion that preceded and was generally supplanted by Christianity in Europe. Pockets of believers in this Old Religion, especially in Britain and Ireland, passed along the secrets to their children and grandchildren. The more prestigious contemporary witches claim descendancy from these first families of witchcraft; but thousands of recent "converts" have no such pedigree.

Related to witchcraft are the various neopagan cults, such as the Druids. In ancient times the term "pagan" was applied to rural people in contrast to the people living in cities and towns, who were more likely to have embraced Christianity. It had about the same meaning as "hick" or "rube" in today's parlance. Those who identify themselves as contemporary pagans usually practice a type of nature-religion with an emphasis on hedonism.

People dabble in witchcraft for a variety of reasons. Some are attracted by the promise of witchcraft to endow the practitioners with the power to cast spells, win lovers, cure warts, discomfort enemies, and otherwise accomplish their wishes by magical means. Young people sometimes take up witchcraft as a new "kick," a way to "turn on" without drugs through mysterious rites, nudity, incantations, incense, dancing, and other such carryings-on. To the "born" witches, such conversions bring the satisfaction that witchcraft is being more widely propagated; but their enthusiasm is tempered by the fact that the kids usually do not engage in "top-drawer witchcraft."

The basic unit or congregation of those involved in witchcraft is the *coven* of 13 people. Led by a high priest or high priestess, the coven includes regular witches as well as initiates who may spend from six months to a year to gain full membership. Like Freemasonry, witchcraft has three basic degrees of rank.

With no accrediting body or denominational authority, witchcraft cannot control the formation of covens. Anybody can start a coven; some organizers are serious students of the occult, while others are sports who relish the idea of 13 men and women convorting in the altogether.

Coven members meet at the fortnightly Esbath (or Witches' Sabbath), on a Saturday night around midnight. They also gather for the Old Religion's four main holidays: February 2, April 30, July 31, and, of course, October 31 (Halloween).

Witches worship the Mother Goddess Diana and the Horned God, the chief dieties of the Old Religion. They believe in living a life of easygoing hedonism, followed by death and reincarnation. Witches deny the existence of a devil, so they should be distinguished from the Satanists.

Ususally the high priest or priestess provides the meeting-place in his or her home and prepares it for the esoteric rites. An altar is set up and covered with a white cloth. The ceremonies themselves are conducted inside a consecrated circle drawn in chalk or sand on the floor, and about nine feet in diameter. Candles illuminate the room, and four red candles are often placed in the corners. One object of worship is a reliquary holding a semiprecious stone and the name of the god to whom a particular coven gives its homage. Other witchcraft paraphernalia include a wand and sword, a plate of salt, a goblet of water, incense, and a broom; the last is understood as the symbol of domestic cleanliness rather than as the witches' mode of transportation.

Witches greet each other with "Blessed be." Clothes are supposed to hamper their mystical vibrations, so they usually shed their garments and conduct their activities in the nude (or "skyclad"). Some covens practice their rituals in long robes with nothing worn underneath. The rituals themselves are recorded in the witchcraft bible, called the Book of Shadows. Copies are handwritten by initiates and kept out of the hands of the profane.

In addition to the nudity, the sexual element in witchcraft is obvious. At an initiation, the high priest kneels in front of the candidate and bestows the fivefold kiss on the feet, knees, sexual organs, breasts, and lips. Much of the ritual of the Old Religion is made up simply of phallic worship and fertility rites.

The candidate for full membership repeats the following oath: *I, _____, in the presence of the mighty One, do of my own free will and accord most solemnly swear that I will ever keep secret and never reveal the secrets of the art, except be it to a proper person, properly prepared within a circle such as I am now in. All this I swear by my hopes of a future life mindful that my measure has been taken and may my weapons turn against me if I break this solemn oath.*

Hans Holzer, author of *The Truth about Witchcraft* (1969) and many other books on the occult, reports that the majority of witches he knows are former Roman Catholics. The high priest of a London coven that allowed him to witness an initiation is a defrocked, thrice-married Catholic priest. Holzer comments: "I have never met a former Unitarian or other liberal Christian who sought out witchcraft, simply because the liberal Christian churches are close enough to the ideals of the Craft not to warrant it."

Witches do not believe in heaven, hell, or the devil; but almost all accept the doctrine of reincarnation. They view Satanism as a perversion of Christianity and have nothing to do with devil-worship or Black Masses. At least they don't if they consider themselves "white" witches (rather than "black" witches, who specialize in curses and mischief making).

Some witches view magic as supernatural, but the majority of contemporary witches prefer to see magic as "supernormal." They maintain that magic works, but do not attempt to explain why it works.

The experienced witch has a spell for almost every situation. For example, if a burglar has broken into your house and you do not want him to return, you can ask your neighborhood witch to cast a spell. For this she (or he) needs three pieces of hog fat, three pieces of salt. The witch throws these items into an open fire and recites the appropriate incantation. If the spell works, you will not be bothered by a burglar again.

But spells can work both good or evil. If you were the burglar, you might consult your own witch, probably a black witch, who would cast a spell to facilitate your endeavor. She would ask the gods to muzzle the householder's watchdog, let the householder enjoy a deep sleep, or let you escape with your loot.

Ethical witches may disown black magic and Satanism, but these do count some adherents. For example, Anton Szandor LaVey directs the First Church of Satan in San Francisco. A former circus lion-tamer, LaVey wears a black robe and clerical collar; he has shaved his head but wears a mustache and goatee, which give him an alleged resemblance to the Master he claims to serve. He frankly identifies himself as the devil's advocate. Like Milton's fallen angel, the Satanists believe it is "better to rule in Hell than serve in Heaven."

Satan's clergyman schedules a Black Mass every Friday at midnight at his church. A genuine Black Mass calls for a defrocked priest, consecrated host, a prostitute, and a virgin whose body serves as an altar. LaVey's imitation falls short on most of these criteria, as do the Black Masses of assorted underground groups who encounter difficulties in finding a qualified "altar."

LaVey has conducted weddings and funerals at his "church" and apparently meets the legal requirements of the state as an ordained minister. He claims that more than 7,000 people in 25 "grottoes" around the country pay a $13 membership fee in his Satanic denomination.

He maintains that Satanism is simply the belief that human beings should gratify every desire so long as they do not hurt others. "It's just Ayn Rand's philosophy with ceremony and ritual added," explains the Reverend LaVey.

One student of the occult, Prof. Marcello Truzzi, classified white witches as falling under various subtypes: Traditional, Murrayite, Eclectic, Gardnerian, Alexandrian, Continental, and so forth. He identifies black witches as including Traditional Satanists, Acid-culture Eclectic Satanists, Heretical Anti-Catholic Satanists, members of the Church of Satan, and Baphometists. Both witchcraft and Satanism are fragmented but jealous of their claims to represent the true faith.

CHAPTER III

Jehovah's Witnesses

*They have been predicting the end of the world
for 100 years.*

Many of the well known contemporary cults concentrate their recruiting on or near the nation's college campuses. A few gain notoriety by pestering travelers at airports or importuning passersby at shopping centers. Jehovah's Witnesses (Watchtower Society) go door-to-door trying to warn their neighbors about the end of the world and seeking converts. They have assigned your house and your neighborhood to some Witness who is expected to call on you once or twice a year.

All Jehovah's Witnesses are expected to make a fundamental commitment to propagate their doctrines. The Watchtower Society constantly prods the Witnesses to spare no time or effort to warn their neighbors about the impending, climactic Battle of Armageddon. The world as we know it will soon end. Tomorrow may be too late to cast your lot with Jehovah.

Worldwide the number of Witnesses now exceeds 2 million, and of these about 530,000 are Americans. In 1942 the total membership was only 106,000. The Watchtower Society has been a growth institution.

Once a year the Witnesses hold a Memorial Service. At this annual communion celebration, only about 10,000 come forward to partake of the bread and wine—thereby indicating that they believe themselves to belong to the 144,000 who will reign in heaven with Jesus Christ. The total attendance includes not only full-fledged Witnesses but people preparing for baptism or sympathetic to the movement. In a recent year, almost 5 million people attended the service.

The Society makes no provision for inactive or honorary members. One who simply contributes a few dollars and attends an occasional Kingdom Hall meeting has no status in the Society. Even bedridden Witnesses are urged to write letters or telephone people to spread the message. Children too are expected to do their share; many youngsters give up baseball and TV to accompany their parents as they go door-to-door selling copies of the *Watchtower* or trying to sign up householders for a Bible class.

What kind of a commitment does a baptized Witness make? A typical week might go something like this: On Sunday morning the Witness may spend several hours in doorstep preaching; the sect expects each member to log at least 10 hours a month in such work. Another couple of hours on Sunday may be devoted to studying the current issue of *Watchtower*. Later in the day the Witnesses go to their Kingdom Hall for a public lecture and *Watchtower* meeting, which together last two hours. On Monday the Witness prepares for a Bible-study class and may rehearse an eight-minute sermon to be delivered later in the week. Tuesday evening is given over to a congregational book-study. On Wednesday or Thursday the Witness goes back to Kingdom Hall for the Theocratic Ministry School and the Service Meeting. Householders who have shown any interest in the sect's literature get a return call on Friday. Finally on Saturday the Witness may again set out to distribute copies of the *Watchtower* (or its companion magazine, *Awake!*).

Most Witnesses also hold secular jobs and have family responsibilities. The 16 to 20 hours demanded by the sect leave little extra time during the week and almost mandates a withdrawal from secular society. This result suits the purposes of the Watchtower Society, in whose eyes the world is a sinful, doomed place anyway.

Converts to the sect find their whole life revolving around the activities of Kingdom Hall; their friendships with non-Witnesses begin to wither. They will neither vote in civic or national elections nor run for public office. They can retain a passive membership in a labor union but are warned not to become involved in union politics, strikes, or picketing. The Witnesses will not join a lodge or social organization or squander precious hours watching TV, playing cards, dancing, or attending the movies. This New World Society asks for nothing less than total commitment.

In some respects the typical Witness would be classified as a religious fanatic. But the typical Catholic or Protestant pastor would be delighted to find even a tenth of the congregation willing to devote as much time, effort, and study as do those who gather weekly at a Kingdom Hall. In point of fact, most of those who now center their lives on Kingdom Hall once worshiped in Catholic or Protestant churches. Relatively few Witnesses come from Witness families or non-church backgrounds.

Despite the enormous demands the Watchtower Society makes of its members — not to mention the active persecution of them in Communist and other countries — the movement displays a remarkable record of growth.

Most Christian magazines never reach a circulation of 100,000; the largest, *Columbia,* goes to the homes of 1,200,000 Knights of Columbus. But the *Watchtower* reports a press run of 9,200,000 copies per issue, in 82 languages. The circulation of *Awake!* is about the same.

When the Watchtower Bible and Tract Society publishes a new hardbound book, it starts with a first edition of 2,500,000 copies. It asks a donation of 50 cents for a 380-page book. Witnesses write the book, set the type, run the presses, and operate the bindery. One of the Society's doctrinal texts has become the fourth-largest bestseller of all time with 74 million copies in print. Only the Bible, *Quotations from Chairman Mao,* and the *American Spelling Book* by Noah Webster have seen more copies in print than *The Truth That Leads to Eternal Life.*

In just 100 years, the Watchtower Society has grown to 42,000 congregations in some 200 countries. Few religious groups have grown so fast.

It all began when a young Pittsburgh haberdasher began to rummage through the Bible, especially the Books of Daniel and Revelation. Charles Taze Russell (1852-1916) had been raised a Congregationalist but had drifted into agnosticism. A chance visit to an Adventist meeting sparked in him a new interest in the Bible.

Interest in Adventism among American Protestants had already begun to wane by the time Russell came to accept the idea of an imminent Second Coming. Several decades earlier William Miller had attracted thousands of followers by claiming that the Bible predicted that the end of the world would come in 1843 or 1844. When these years passed without incident, most Millerites withdrew from the movement in disillusionment. A remnant led by the prophetess Ellen G. White formed the Seventh-day Adventist Church.

Russell lacked even a high-school education, but he managed to master the use of Hebrew and Greek dictionaries. His interpretations of biblical passages flatly contradicted the beliefs of orthodox Christianity. For example, he denied the existence of hell and the doctrine of the Trinity. In his 19th-century version of the Arian heresy, he taught that only God the Father (Jehovah) is God, that Jesus is a creature, and that the Holy Spirit was not a person at all but a name for the power of God. God created Jesus, who was also known in heaven as Michael the Archangel. Jesus became a man, taught, died as a ransom for all people, and was raised as a mighty spirit-creature to serve as God's executive officer in heaven.

Russell apparently thought that the churches would welcome his scriptural discoveries and was offended when pulpits were closed to him. He started his own Bible classes, began publication of the *Watch Tower and Herald of Christ's Presence* (1879), and launched what would eventually become known as Jehovah's Witnesses.

Russell assumed the title "Pastor," by which he was known to his supporters. He traveled around the world preaching his novel biblical interpretations and prophecies. From his pen flowed a stream of books, tracts, and magazine articles. In 1908 he moved his headquarters from Pittsburgh to Brooklyn.

Some of his followers left after his highly publicized marital problems. Maria Russell, his wife, who was also active in the movement and helped edit the publications, sued for divorce on grounds of "his conceit, egotism, domination, and improper conduct in relation to other women." The Pastor was later returned to court several times when he tried to avoid alimony payments. Other disciples turned away when he tried to promote a $60-a-bushel "Miracle Wheat," a fake cancer cure, and a marvelous Millenial Bean.

The year 1914 came and passed, and, contrary to Pastor Russell's prediction, the end of the world had not yet come. He went back to his study of the Bible and then announced that what he had expected to be a visible event had really been invisible. Christ and Satan had battled in heaven, and Satan had been thrown down to the vicinity of the earth to continue his mischief. This event was said to account for the wars and revolutions, famines, earthquakes, epidemics, and other disasters that commenced in or after 1914.

Pastor Russell died in 1916 on a Pullman car while returning from a preaching trip to the West Coast. His followers then numbered only a few thousand.

A shrewd country lawyer succeeded Pastor Russell. "Judge" Joseph R. Rutherford (1869-1942) had left the Baptist church of his family in Missouri and joined the Watchtower staff as legal adviser. He outfoxed his rivals to gain control of the Society, though some dissidents formed minor schismatic groups — the Dawn Bible Students Association and the Layman's Home Missionary Movement, to name two. At first Rutherford could not say enough in praise of Pastor Russell. "When the history of the Church of Christ is fully written, it will be found that the place next to St. Paul in the gallery of fame as expounders of the Gospel of the great master will be occupied by Charles Taze Russell."

In a few years, however, the new president set out to destroy the cult of personality that had grown up around the memory of Russell. Rutherford let Russell's books go out of print. He discarded some of the Pastor's pet theories, such as one concerning the Great Pyramid. Today the name of Russell is barely known among Jehovah's Witnesses, and many of his teachings have become only a source of embarrassment to the cult's hierarchy.

Rutherford and other top officers of the Society were imprisoned for a time in the Atlanta penitentiary on charges of sedition, but were released after the passions of World War I had cooled. They found that the schisms, the war, and the prison terms had reduced Watchtower membership; by 1920, only 9,000 remained in the organization.

Judge Rutherford set about to rebuild the organization. He coined the slogan "Millions Now Living Will Never Die" and, in 1931, bestowed a new name on the cult: Jehovah's Witnesses. (The sect had previously been known as Russellites, Millenial Dawnists, and International Bible Students.) He equipped his followers with portable phonographs so that they could play his recorded sermonettes to prospective converts in living rooms. Russell's on-going feud with the main-line churches became a more prominent feature of the cult during the Rutherford regime. Zealous Witnesses paraded in front of Catholic and Protestant churches on Sunday mornings carrying placards proclaiming "RELIGION IS A SNARE AND A RACKET."

Rutherford displayed a particular hatred toward Catholicism and intensified his attacks on the Church by means of radio sermons and lurid pamphlets. The reputation for orneriness that still is associated with the movement is largely a legacy of Rutherford's 25 years as president. After his death (1942), the Watchtower Society underwent a considerable face-lifting, which has tempered the crude attacks on the Catholic and Protestant churches. The basic hostility of the cult toward organized religion still remains.

In 1920 Rutherford had predicted, "We may confidently expect that 1925 will mark the return of Abraham, Isaac, Jacob, and the faithful prophets of old." He spent most of his declining years in a mansion near San Diego, which the cult had purchased as an abode for the Old Testament Princes who were soon to return to earth. He seldom appeared at Witness rallies or meetings but continued to produce numerous Scripture-laden books and pamphlets until his death. (The mansion was later sold.)

The cantankerous tactics of many Witnesses made more enemies than converts, but the number of active Witnesses grew tenfold during the Rutherford years. World War II disrupted the cult's missionary activity. Hundreds of Jehovah's Witnesses died in concentration camps, and thousands endured prison terms in both Axis and Allied countries for refusing military service.

The third head of the Watchtower Society, Nathan Homer Knorr (1905-1977), joined the movement as a teenager. Soon after his high-school graduation, he started to work in the cult's printing plant at the Brooklyn headquarters. A man of obvious organizational abilities, he soon perceived that many of Rutherford's methods (including the recorded sermonettes) had outlived their usefulness. Knorr set up a public-speaking course for all Witnesses so that they could deliver their own testimonies. He muted the obnoxious anticlericalism of the 1940s without shedding his belief that organized religion, business, and government formed an evil triumvirate. Knorr also established a school to prepare foreign missionaries and sect leaders.

Knorr chose an anonymous committee of Witnesses to produce a new translation of the Bible. The first of the six volumes of the *New World Translation of the Hebrew and Christian Greek Scriptures* appeared in 1950; the sixth volume was published 11 years later. In Kingdom Halls and in their personal study, the Witnesses use their own translation; but in talking to householders they will make use of more familiar versions.

Throughout their translation, the Witnesses tried to buttress their own teachings by various devices. For example, where other translations use "Lord" or "God," the New World translation substitutes "Jehovah." Denying the divinity of Jesus Christ, the Witness translators render "the Word was God" as "the Word was a god" (John 1.1). Prof. Anthony Hoekema of Calvin College has written that "their New World Translation of the Bible is by no means an objective rendering of the sacred text into modern English but is a biased translation in which many of the peculiar teachings of the Watchtower Society are smuggled into the text of the Bible itself" *(The Four Major Cults*, pp. 238-239).

Since hardly any college graduates belonged to the Watchtower Society in 1950, the translation committee was probably made up of high-school graduates with access to Greek and Hebrew dictionaries. In this they would be following the tradition established by Pastor Russell. Their product, the New World Translation, has no value in the eyes of scripture scholars.

When Knorr died in 1977, the self-perpetuating Watchtower hierarchy chose an 83-year-old bachelor, Frederick Franz, as his successor. Franz is the first head of the Society to have attended college; he dropped out of the University of Cincinnati during his junior year and has lived at Brooklyn headquarters since 1920. For decades he has been regarded as the sect's leading theologian.

He took over the reins of the Society at an awkward time. For some years, *Watchtower* and *Awake!* had pointed to 1975 as the probable date for Armageddon. Witnesses have believed that Adam was created in the autumn of 4026 B.C., which meant that the allotted 6,000 years of human existence would end in late 1975. This period would be followed by the Millenium. When Armageddon did not occur in 1975, Franz had to explain that the seventh day of creation did not begin until Eve was created. Nowadays Witnesses do not reveal the interval between the creation of Adam and that of Eve, but they previously had reported that the two had been created in the same year.

Disappointment over the false alarm in 1975 has reduced the Society's membership and number of baptisms. For the first time since World War II, the U.S. membership declined; the Society's 1978 *Yearbook* reveals a drop of 2.6 percent from 1977, to 530,373 members. Also the number of convert baptisms in the U.S. dropped 65 percent during the years 1976-77. For almost two decades after 1958, the number of Witnesses had risen 5 percent a year in the U.S.

Even a modest drop in the membership upsets the cult's leadership, for the Watchtower's amazing membership gains have been used as evidence of Jehovah's satisfaction with the Society. They tend to ignore the fact that the Mormons, Seventh-day Adventists, Communists, Pentecostals, Muslims, and other groups and sects also registered considerable growth during the 1960s and 1970s.

No Jehovah's Witness in the 1980s is encouraged to study the writings of either Russell or Rutherford. Now all books and magazine articles are published anonymously. Witnesses consider the Watchtower Society to be Jehovah's representative on earth and do not criticize its theology, policies, or appointments.

Jehovah's Witnesses can fairly be called fundamentalist unitarians. Their theology shows the influence also of adventism, universalism, and the beliefs of the tiny Christadelphian sect. Their approach to the Bible is literal; their apologetic method has been to assemble as many proof-texts as possible to sustain a particular doctrinal position, while ignoring context or texts that might challenge their interpretation. They are unitarian in that they deny that Jesus is the second person of the Trinity and that the Holy Spirit refers to a person at all.

Their beliefs can be summarized thus:

In the beginning was Jehovah. He created Jesus (Michael), and the two then became co-creators of everything else. Pastor Russell estimated that the creation of the world took place about 6,000 years ago, but present-day Witnesses calculate that the material universe is 48,000 years old. Jehovah appointed an angel to watch over the planet earth, but the angel grew jealous of Jehovah, seduced Adam and Eve, and became Satan. Jehovah accepted Satan's challenge that the latter could win over all people, but gave him only 6,000 years to accomplish his objective. If Satan fails, the Witnesses believe, Jehovah will re-establish his kingdom and destroy Satan and all his cohorts.

Abel is regarded as the first Jehovah's Witness, and each of the prophets of the Old Testament also bore this title. Likewise "all Christians in the first-century congregations were Witnesses of Jehovah" (*Jehovah's Witnesses in the Divine Purpose*, p. 9).

After thousands of years of Satan's rule, Jehovah sent his only son to become a man and ransom people from sin. After Jesus was killed on a torture stake — not a cross — he was raised up as a spirit-creature.

The final battle between Jehovah and Satan will occur during the lifetime of those alive in 1914, certainly during the next eight to ten years. Besides the 144,000 who will live in heaven, other Jehovah's Witnesses will live forever in a paradise on earth, no longer fearing sickness, death, old age, or evil. The wicked and stubborn unbelievers will simply be annihilated.

Although eschatology occupies a paramount place in the sect's theology, the unusual biblical interpretations of the Watchtower Society affect the lives of all adherents. The Society condemns the celebration of birthdays, the use of hypnosis, the observance of Christmas and Easter, the United Nations, Protestant and Catholic churches, military service, flag saluting, gambling, the teaching of evolution, Mother's Day, tobacco, and higher education, among other things.

A Witness may belong to a labor union, but the *Watchtower* warns that "a Christian should not get involved in union activity to the extent of holding an official position in the union. Nor, in the event of a strike, should he take part in picketing or in other ways agitate for the cause of the strike. . . . Just as a Christian is neutral regarding politics and wars of his country, so the union member who is a Christian does not get involved in the governing activities and economic warfare of the union but must remain neutral" *(Watchtower,* Feb. 15, 1961, p. 128).

Perhaps the Watchtower attitude forbidding members to undergo blood transfusions has caused more problems and publicity than the cult's other taboos. The Society interprets Genesis 9.4 and Leviticus 7.26 as forbidding such procedures. All other biblical scholars have understood the prohibition of the "eating of blood" to refer to drinking blood rather than to any medical technique unknown in ancient days.

A Jehovah's Witness who accepts a blood transfusion or allows his or her child to receive a transfusion will be disfellowshipped. Such a person may attend Kingdom Hall meetings but may not speak or be spoken to by anyone. The penalty may be lifted after a year. A Witness may incur the same penalty for obtaining a divorce on any grounds except adultery; for drunkenness; or for attending a Protestant or Catholic church. Fraternizing with non-Witnesses save for the purpose of trying to convert them is also frowned upon.

Most denominations welcome converts, and some make systematic efforts to attract new members. But Jehovah's Witnesses put an extraordinary emphasis on growth. The sect's *Yearbook* and periodicals regularly publicize the number of baptisms, the hours spent in doorstep preaching, the number of Bibles and books printed, and the percentage increase of Witness publishing in various countries. Any decline in activity brings admonitions to do better the following year.

Each Kingdom Hall has an assigned missionary area, and each Witness has a territory to cover. The work is not left to chance. Decades of experience have gone into the formulation of the Seven Steps involved in the Society's proselytizing:

Step 1 is to get a copy of the *Watchtower* or a pamphlet into the hands of the prospective convert. A typical opening when someone answers the doorbell might be: "How would you like to live in a world without sickness, war, poverty, or any other problems?" Like life insurance or encyclopedia salespeople, the Witnesses try to elicit several positive answers to start the conversation.

If the householder buys or accepts a magazine, Step 2 is to arrange a "back call" to encourage study of the material.

Step 3 is to invite the person to a Bible study in the home of another Witness. These study sessions are anything but open and free discussions of the Scriptures; an experienced Witness directs the study according to prescribed Watchtower guidelines.

Participation in an *area* Bible study follows the home-study session, as Step 4.

Step 5 brings the prospect inside the local Kingdom Hall. At one time the Witnesses met in storefronts and rented rooms, but now the congregation may own a modest building that can seat 100 to 300 people. Its interior resembles that of a classroom more than that of a church. At the Kingdom Hall, the prospective convert gets the VIP treatment. The newcomer notices that "Brother" and "Sister" are the usual forms of address. Here are people who care about one another, who introduce the newcomer to other people, who seem confident and assured about what they believe.

Getting the prospect to attend the Service meeting on a Wednesday or Thursday night is Step 6. The mid-week meeting resembles a sales meeting in a business. Congregation officials give tips on how to improve door-to-door preaching, tally the number of calls made and pamphlets placed, and record the hours logged by members.

By this time, the man or woman who answered the doorbell months ago has been drawn further into the Watchtower organization. The prospect has made new friends and has probably been encouraged to accompany an older Witness on rounds. The last and 7th Step remains: regular attendance at all the weekly meetings and finally baptism (by immersion). In 1978, about 95,000 people took this final step.

Once committed to the New World Society, the Witness finds that his or her social life, sexual standards, time, attitude toward secular society, and personal relationships are now determined by the Watchtower Society. Obviously the total dedication demanded by the new faith can put a severe strain on a marriage if only one spouse becomes a Jehovah's Witness.

The Watchtower Society tolerates its members' drinking an occasional glass of beer but condemns smoking as a defilement of the flesh. Cigarette addiction will prevent a Witness from advancement in the congregation. The demands on the Witness's time are such that TV-watching, movies, dancing, card playing, hobbies, recreational reading, and the like are usually supplanted by religious activities.

The Society inculcates a strict sexual morality. An unmarried Witness who engages in sexual intercourse risks expulsion from the congregation, as does an adulterer or philanderer. Masturbation is considered wicked. The Society leaves the choice of birth-control methods up to the married couple but takes a strong position against abortion and sterilization: "Abortion is a violation of God's law against killing" *(Awake!,* Dec. 8, 1964). During Rutherford's era, the Society urged members to forego marriage to devote more time to preaching; but celibacy is no longer set up as an ideal. Milton G. Henschel, a member of the Society's governing body, has stated that "no homosexuals are permitted to be members of the congregations of Jehovah's Witnesses" (quoted in Leo Rosten's *Religions of America,* p. 140).

Witnesses consider themselves citizens of Jehovah's New World Society rather than of any secular state. As such they claim exemption from military service, as would any ambassador of a foreign nation. Their stance toward the state explains their refusal to salute the flag, stand for recitation of the national anthem, vote, or hold public office. They are not pacifists like the Quakers or Amish. They eagerly await the greatest battle in history, Armageddon, and would gladly serve Jehovah with arms if he asked for their help in his fight with Satan.

Such movements as ecumenism and women's liberation leave the Watchtower Society untouched. All positions of leadership in Kingdom Halls, as well as at the cult's headquarters in Brooklyn, are held by men. Henschel explains, "Women may share in our congregational Bible studies and meetings, but they would never enter into debate with men in the congregation, challenging them" (p. 139). A woman might temporarily assume a leadership role in a tiny congregation, but she would be replaced by the first qualified man who joined the congregation.

Some Witnesses devote all or most of their time to the work of the Society. A Regular Pioneer is expected to spend 100 hours a month in Watchtower work and support himself with a part-time job; a Special Pioneer devotes at least 150 hours and receives a small salary.

A Jehovah's Witness congregation employs no full-time ministers. The elders select a presiding minister to serve a one-year term; he has authority to baptize, officiate at weddings and funerals, and so on. Other local officials include an assistant presiding minister, ministerial assistants, and elders. Beyond the individual congregations are the circuit overseers, who supervise about 15 Kingdom Halls each and are usually selected from the ranks of the Special Pioneers. These are full-time, salaried positions. A district overseer looks after about a dozen circuits, and a branch committee directs the work of the movement in a particular country or territory. All positions are held by men, appointed or ratified by authorities of the Watchtower Society in Brooklyn.

Although segregated Kingdom Halls used to be common in the South, the Witnesses now have a good record for practicing racial equality. As many as 20 percent of American Witnesses are blacks; they are not allowed, of course, to participate in the NAACP or any civil-rights groups. The sect has also registered significant gains in Spanish-speaking communities.

The size of the typical Kingdom Hall is deliberately small. Once a congregation reaches 200 members, plans are made to establish an offshoot congregation. Whereas the average Catholic parish in the United States includes about 1,800 people, the average Kingdom Hall has only 75.

About 2,000 Witnesses (including Frederick Franz) live and work at worldwide headquarters in Brooklyn; another 600 live on a Watchtower farm in upstate New York. All receive the same recompense: room, board, and $25 a month allowance. These residents of Bethel set the printer's type and run the presses, administer the organization, and conduct the five-month courses at Gilead for missionaries. The Society maintains other large printing plants in Canada, England, West Germany, South Africa, and Scandinavia.

Because many congregations are small in number, and the individual Witness may consequently feel isolated, the Society regularly arranges rallies in various cities. As many as 252,000 Witnesses have attended a rally in New York City. Not only do the assemblies promote fellowship and esprit de corps, but they also serve as occasions for introducing new Watchtower books and policies and for generating publicity. News reports often comment on the tight organization of these rallies, the politeness of the visitors, and the clean-up efforts that leave the stadiums in better shape than ever. In 1978 the cult scheduled 100 conventions in 45 countries.

The Watchtower Society operates *no* hospitals, clinics, sanitariums, grade or high schools, colleges, old people's homes, orphanages, or social-welfare agencies. The Witnesses reason that since the world will soon be destroyed, such services could not do much good. (In contrast, the Seventh-day Adventists, who also see the end of the world as nigh, support an extensive parochial-school system and a health-care network around the world.)

The largest contingent of Witnesses are Americans, but most Witnesses live outside the United States. Some of the larger groups are in Nigeria (114,000), Brazil (106,000), West Germany (102,000), Mexico (84,000), the British Isles (80,000), and the Philippines (77,000). When religious liberty was granted in Spain in 1970, the Witnesses gained legal recognition and now say they are the second-largest denomination in the country (*Awake!*, Dec. 8, 1976). Though Communist countries ban Witness activities, the Watchtower Society estimates that it has about 185,000 members in such countries.

In a number of emerging nations, the Witnesses' outspoken anti-state and pacifist position collides with militant nationalism. African countries that have recently thrown off colonial rule find it hard to accommodate a group of people who refuse to serve in the army, will not vote, prefer jail to saluting the flag, and claim citizenship in the Theocracy instead of the state. The Witnesses have faced persecution in Zambia and Malawi. An estimated 22,000 Jehovah's Witnesses were driven from Malawi in 1973 after the government banned the sect.

Brooklyn officials said 60 Witnesses died during the rout. The president of Malawi explained, "The Jehovah's Witnesses asked for it. They would not pay taxes, recognize the flag, or sing the national anthem. So we just prohibited them because they were a nuisance. And they were rude. They don't believe in government at all, only in God."

In late 1976, Argentina's ruling military junta closed down Watchtower headquarters in Buenos Aires and forbade all Witness work. The junta declared that the 35,000 Witnesses were a living affront to the principles of nationhood.

By standing apart from any but the most necessary contacts with governments, the Witnesses risk persecution; but they also thereby exert a powerful appeal for those who distrust any and all politicians and political institutions.

Armageddon has been predicted for 1914 and 1925 and 1975, but the indefatigable Jehovah's Witnesses insist it is still just around the corner. The Society's growth has been lagging in recent years, but for decades the movement started by Pastor Russell some hundred years earlier has registered membership gains larger than those of any of the main-line Christian churches.

CHAPTER IV

The Self-Realization Fellowship

An Indian guru introduced Hinduism
to thousands of Americans in the 1920s.

Decades before the Hindu sect of the Hare Krishnas attracted any attention, a yogi by the name of Paramahansa Yogananda had brought another interpretation of Hinduism to America.

Yogananda first arrived in the U.S. in 1920 to participate in the International Congress of Religious Liberals, in Boston; the Congress was sponsored by the Unitarian Church. Three years earlier, he had founded the Yogoda Satsanga Society in his native India.

Born Mukunda Lal Ghosh, he was a Bengali and the son of a well-to-do railroad executive. He received a degree from Calcutta University in 1914 and had earlier undergone a period of spiritual training under his own guru. The year he graduated from college he joined a monastic order, and he eventually founded a small school for boys.

The Hindu movement with which he was affiliated originated in 1851. It was based on the Kriya Yoga system of concentration, meditation, and exercise. Through the practice of yoga, the individual is reputedly able to reach spiritual enlightenment and escape from the pursuit of materialism.

Yogananda called his Westernized version of this teaching the Self-Realization Fellowship (or SRF). He maintained that his teaching combined the truths of yoga and of genuine Christianity. He would spend more than 30 years in the U.S.

The yogi bought a 60-room hotel atop Mount Washington in Los Angeles, and this site became headquarters for the movement. Here and in public lectures throughout the country, he instructed devotees in Kriya Yoga and his own blend of Hinduism and Christianity.

In 1932, Yogananda found a wealthy supporter in James F. Lynn, who had acquired a fortune in business and insurance in Kansas City. Lynn mastered yoga and SRF doctrines and became head of the cult when Yogananda died, in 1952. Newspaper accounts reported that the yogi's body showed no sign of corruption even 20 days after his death, when the casket was closed. Lynn contributed $1 million to the SRF in 1953 and bequeathed another $1 million along with a portfolio of stocks.

The present head of the sect was born Faye Wright, and was raised as a Mormon, in Salt Lake City. She joined the Self-Realization Fellowship in 1930 and became a nun. As Sister Daya Mata, she became president of the SRF when Lynn died in 1955. She presides over a governing board of eight, all of whom have spent at least 20 years in the SRF.

Nine of the 44 U.S. congregations are located in California; there are another 100 or so branches in Canada, Mexico, Argentina, Switzerland, India, Australia, and other countries. Ministers are known as Meditation Counselors.

The headquarters complex in Los Angeles includes a convent for nuns, an ashram for monks, an office building, and a printing plant. The last puts out the *Self-Realization Magazine,* books, and pamphlets. The SRF Lake Shrine, on 12 acres in Pacific Palisades, was opened to the public in 1950.

The Fellowship enrolls both laity and "renunciants." The latter practice Kriya Yoga, spend at least two hours a day in meditation, and have completed a lengthy training session. These monks and nuns devote their lives to the work of the order and to self-improvement. They take vows of celibacy, simplicity, obedience, and loyalty.

The cult's vegetarian restaurants in Hollywood and San Diego attract members and non-members. Devotees come to the SRF retreat house on the ocean's shore at Encinitas, California, for meditation and spiritual instruction. The renunciants send healing vibration by prayer to those who seek help from disease, mental inharmonies, and spiritual ignorance.

Worship in one of the SRF churches is based on the meditation practices taught by the yogi. "Meditation, to be most effective, should be scientific as well as devotional. Self-Realization Fellowship Church teaches ancient, proven techniques of yoga for higher results in meditation. As nonsectarian as mathematics, the soul science of yoga may be employed by Christian, Hebrew, or any other religionist to achieve the purpose of all true seekers — a tranforming, joyous experience of the One Lord." The SRF pamphlet in which these words appear also states, "We pray to God and to Jesus Christ and to the saints of all religions" (*Welcome to Self-Realization Church,* p. 4). Instead of hymns, the congregation sings chants, most of which were composed by Paramahansa Yogananda. Novice meditators are told to sit upright and still. They are then told: "Fix your whole attention at the space between the eyebrows, looking up at that point." The SRF teaches that "the spot between the eyebrows is the seat of concentration in the body" (p. 11).

The frequent references to Jesus, to the Christian saints, and to the Bible set the SRF apart from other Hindu sects (such as the International Society for Krishna Consciousness and the Vedanta Society). The SRF explains that it "transcends identification with particular faiths by its service to members of all religions of the World." The SRF does, however, elaborate particularly on the fundamental points of unity between "Christianity, the great religion of the West, and Yoga, the great spiritual science of the East" (*Why a Church of All Religions?*, p. 2).

Yogananda's *Autobiography of a Yogi* remains a perennial bestseller, as does his *Whispers from Eternity*. The SRF probably counts several thousand devotees in the U.S.

CHAPTER V

The Worldwide Church of God

*Herbert W. Armstrong tells followers that
the One, True Church was re-established in 1933.*

Going into the 1970s, the Worldwide Church of God (WCG) seemed to be sitting on top of the world. Through radio, television, and the printed word, it was reaching an estimated 150 million people each year. Garner Ted Armstrong, son of the founder of the cult, attracted an audience numbered in the millions through his weekly programs. The cult's handsome magazine, *Plain Truth,* was mailed free to some 2 million homes. Ambassador College occupied a beautiful campus in posh Pasadena and enrolled nearly 1,000 students, while others attended WCG colleges in Texas and England. A national religious magazine called the WCG "the fastest growing church in America."

By 1980, all had changed. Herbert W. Armstrong had excommunicated his son, Garner Ted, who then moved to Texas and founded the rival Church of God, International. Earlier the son and heir apparent had been relieved of church responsibilities because of his philandering habits. A group of 35 dissident ministers had broken away and set up their own church. Financial problems had forced the WCG to sell its properties in Texas and England; Ambassador College was turned into a small seminary. Income dropped, members withdrew, many radio and TV stations cancelled church programs. Finally in 1979 the attorney general of California, accusing the elder Armstrong and his chief aide of pilfering the assets of the church, brought suit and put the church into receivership. In 1980, Herbert W. Armstrong, age 88 and remarried to a divorcee 45 years his junior, kept himself in seclusion in his Tuscon, Arizona, home, while the religious organization he founded in 1933 tried to weather the storm.

Students of comparative religion see the Worldwide Church of God as a mixture of Seventh-day Adventism, Jehovah's Witnesses, Judaism, Mormonism, and British Israelism. The WCG has been described as "an off-shoot of an off-shoot of an off-shoot of the Seventh-day Adventist Church."

The founder and head of the WCG was born in Des Moines in 1892 and was reared in a Quaker home. He liked to read but quit high school after his sophomore year. At the age of 18 he found a job as a copywriter for the *Merchants Trade Journal*. He married a distant cousin, Loma Miller, who was a Methodist and an avid Bible student. Armstrong was wiped out financially in 1920 and moved to the Pacific Northwest, where he went through two more business failures.

Around 1926 Armstrong started to argue with his wife about religion. She insisted that the proper day for worship was Saturday, while he defended Sunday worship. Nevertheless, after a year of household debate and Bible study, Armstrong came around to his wife's point of view. He had also deduced that Jesus was really crucified on Wednesday instead of Friday. Mr. and Mrs. Armstrong then joined a tiny sect known as the Church of God, which advocated both Saturday worship and adventism.

The original Adventist movement was started by William Miller, a veteran of the War of 1812 and a self-taught Bible scholar. When his several predictions of the end of the world failed to come true, most of his followers melted away; but a small band held to the faith. To this basic Adventist position they added the injunction to worship on Saturday instead of Sunday, and to observe the Judaic dietary laws. Their organization was called the Seventh-day Adventist Church, and today it claims a worldwide membership of more than three million.

In 1866, two members of this body, elders B. F. Snook and W. H. Brinkerhoff, left the Iowa conference of the Seventh-day Adventist Church and formed a new sect, which they named the Church of God (Adventist). Headquarters were established in Stanberry, Missouri, in 1900. But a later schism resulted in formation of still another sect called The Church of God (Seventh Day). This is the "off-shoot of an off-shoot" that the Armstrongs joined.

Armstong devoted more and more time to religious work and was ordained by the Church of God. He conducted his first revival in Eugene, Oregon, in 1933. A 100-watt radio station offered free time for local religious programs, and Armstrong delivered his first radio sermon on October 9, 1934. In the same year, Armstrong mimeographed 250 copies of the first issue of *The Plain Truth*.

Armstrong soon abandoned the church which had ordained him and started what he called the Radio Church of God, later renamed the Worldwide Church of God. His talents for copywriting and merchandising, once devoted to business, were now turned to religion. As one WCG writer has explained: "Jesus chose Paul, who was highly educated, for spreading the gospel to the Gentiles. He later raised up Peter Waldo, a successful businessman, to keep His truth alive during the Middle Ages. In these last days *when the Gospel must go around the world,* Jesus chose a man amply trained in the advertising and business fields to shoulder the mission — Herbert W. Armstrong" (*A True History of the True Church,* by Herman L. Hoeh; Ambassador College, 1959, p. 26).

Armstrong drew up a list of seven criteria by which people today can recognize the genuine church established by Jesus but long fallen into apostacy. These are: (1) observance of the Sabbath on Saturday instead of Sunday; (2) observance of Passover and other Jewish feasts; (3) compliance with the Old Testament dietary laws that forbid eating pork and other "unclean" foods; (4) rejection of belief in the doctrine of the Trinity; (5) adult baptism by immersion, valid only if administered by a "true minister of the true Church"; (6) non-involvement in secular governments; and (7) use of the term "Church of God."

Publications of the WCG regularly condemn both Catholic and Protestant churches for teaching "pagan doctrines and practices." Only one religious organization, the Worldwide Church of God, follows the true faith given to the Apostles. The WCG believes that the corruption of the Christian Church began soon after the death of the last Apostle. "The ministers of Satan had wormed their way in, had gained such power that by persecution or political influence they were able to brand the true people of God as heretics and prevent further organized proclaiming of the same Gospel Christ brought from God. For eighteen and one-half centuries that Gospel was not preached" (*The Inside Story of the World Tomorrow Broadcast,* p. 11).

Armstrong has blasted Roman Catholicism as "the great apostate church" but adds that Catholicism's "many Protestant daughters are also Satan's churches" (according to the WCG's official history).

The strongest influence on Armstrong's theology has been Seventh-day Adventism, but other influences also are evident. The WCG preaches that the world is living in the "latter days," shortly before the battle of Armageddon. Like the Adventists, the WCG insists that Saturday is the only day on which God demands worship; the Sunday observance of most other Christian churches thus is held to violate one of the most important commandments. Again, like the Adventists, Armstrong's followers abstain from pork, ham, lobster, clams, and shrimp in accordance with Old Testament prohibitions. The WCG employs the laying-on of hands and anointing with oil for healing but rejects speaking in tongues.

In personal standards the WCG differs from the Seventh-day Adventist Church. Both churches prohibit smoking, but the WCG allows drinking in moderation. An item in the March-April 1972 issue of *The Plain Truth* even recommends wine: "Natural dry red wine (12% alcohol), still in the aging process, is the best therapeutic wine to buy. It is not only healthful, but also an economical gourmet treat when consumed in moderation." While the Adventists operate a medical school and a chain of hospitals and clinics, the members of the Worldwide Church of God are generally discouraged from seeking medical help.

Until 1974 Armstrong demanded that divorced and remarried persons who joined the WCG had to break up their second marriages. Shortly thereafter he married a church secretary who was a divorcee. His first wife had died in 1967, a few months before their golden wedding anniversary.

Baptized members of the WCG are expected to tithe their incomes. Armstrong comments: "This practice has caused members to be more careful in budgeting personal finances. These members have prospered financially and, consequently, so has the Church" (*This Is the Worldwide Church of God*, p. 19).

Not only are WCG members expected to contribute a tithe to the church, but they are asked to contribute a second 10 percent to finance church festivals and, every third year, another 10 percent to help the needy. So every third year, the faithful are expected to donate 30 percent of their income, 20 percent being the norm for intervening years.

In its heyday, annual income of the WCG exceeded $70 million, mostly from tithes. Non-members also make contributions, but no direct solicitation of funds is made in the publications or broadcasts. The tithes and other contributions provide an income at least double that of the Billy Graham organization, and allow Herbert W. Armstrong to commute anywhere in the world in a $3.5 million executive jet.

Though Seventh-day Adventists follow an orthodox Christology, the WCG has adopted a position similar to Jehovah's Witnesses, denying the doctrine of the Trinity. The Holy Spirit, in Armstrong's theology, is spoken of not as a person but as a divine force.

Armstrong teaches that no human being has reached, or ever will reach, heaven, which is reserved for God and his angels. Jesus left heaven to become a man but has now returned there. During the Battle of Armageddon, he will come back to set up a theocracy in Jerusalem and reign eternally on earth.

The WCG describes three resurrections. The first will be of the righteous who have died before the Second Coming. Together with living members of the WCG, they will become the first citizens of the new kingdom. At the end of a millenium, those who never had a chance to hear about Jesus Christ will be resurrected and given that opportunity. The third resurrection will be of short duration for the stubbornly wicked, who will then be annihilated.

From Mormonism, Armstrong appropriated the idea that human beings can aspire to godhood. The theological concept promoted by the WCG is that "God" is a "family" including the Father, Jesus Christ, and the spiritual sons who also become divine. This teaching echoes the Mormon belief: "What man is now God once was; what God is now man may become."

A WCG pamphlet explains: "The Purpose of your being alive is that finally you be born into the Kingdom of God, when you will actually be GOD, even as Jesus was and is God, and His Father, a different Person, also is God" (*Why Were You Born*, p. 21).

Armstrong's group is the most influential exponent of a curious school of biblical interpretation known as British Israelism (or Anglo-Israelism). The fundamental premise of this school is that the ten lost tribes of Israel found their way to northern Europe and became ancestors of the Saxons who invaded England. England then becomes the Israel of the Bible, and all biblical references to Israel now apply to the English. The British Israelists believe that the Queen of England sits on the throne of King David. The coronation Stone of Scone is really the stone Jacob used for a pillow, and allegedly he took it with him when he left Bethel.

The appeal of British Israelism was stronger before World War II than it is today. The achievement of the people of one small island in mastering a large part of the globe was seen as clear evidence of God's favor. The loss of the empire embarrassed the proponents of British Israelism, but the contemporary British Israelists now include the United States along with England in their biblical prophecies.

Two other cult-leaders in America join Armstrong in promoting British Israelism. James Lovell of Fort Worth edits *Kingdom Digest* and brings his message to many via radio. Howard Rand heads Destiny Publishers of Haverhill, Massachusetts, and claims a 23,000 monthly circulation for his magazine.

Many of the estimated 3 million followers of the British Israel theory remain in mainline Protestant denominations. But the theory holds very little credence among most biblical scholars. Armstrong has elaborated his version of British Israelism primarily in two books: *Where Are the Ten Lost Tribes?* and *The United States and British Commonwealth in Prophecy.*

Like Jehovah's Witnesses, the WCG members condemn the celebration of Christmas and Easter as pagan festivals. Unlike the Witnesses, they maintain that Passover and the other Jewish feasts must be observed by all true Christians. "Passover, the days of unleavened bread, Pentecost, and the holy days God has ordained forever were all observed by Jesus" (*Easter Is Pagan*, p. 4).

The requirement to observe the Jewish holidays may also explain the WCG stand on the moderate use of wine.

WCG members steer clear of involvement in secular government. Until 1976 it was considered a sin for a WCG member to vote in a political election; but this position has been modified.

Before its recent troubles, the WCG claimed a membership of about 75,000, gathered in some 250 congregations. Of these, about 50,000 were Americans. Members contributed annual tithes of about $70 million to the WCG headquarters in Pasadena. They generally met in rented halls and hotel rooms and did not welcome visitors. The denomination was served by 350 ordained ministers.

People who sympathize with the movement but have not reached full membership are known as "co-workers"; one of these is chess grand master Bobby Fischer. Unlike a group such as the Unity School of Christianity, of Lee's Summit, Missouri, which projects an ambiguous image (church or publishing house?), the Armstrong movement frankly presents itself as a church—in fact, as the only legitimate Christian church on earth.

Keystone of the Worldwide Church of God was Ambassador College. Herbert Armstrong says that other colleges and universities spend too much time teaching students how to make a living and not enough telling them how to live. He tells his followers that modern education ignores God, rejects the Bible, and instills false, materialistic values.

At one time, 900 students enrolled at the main Pasadena campus, studying the liberal arts, education, and graduate courses in theology. Although not accredited as a four-year college, it offered doctorates in education, philosophy, and theology. The 45-acre campus occupies a choice location in Pasadena. The college has a formal Italian sunken garden, contemporary-style halls for science and fine arts, and several remodeled mansions once occupied by multimillionaires. A brochure assures readers that at Ambassador College there are "no student or faculty revolts, no protest marches, no riots or violence."

Armstrong himself, though lacking a high school diploma, served as chancellor of the California campus, as well as of the branch at St. Albans, England (350 students) and that at Big Sandy, Texas (550 students).

The WCG communications center in Pasadena includes a completely equipped TV studio, a $2.5 million computer, and a huge printing plant. Three four-color web presses turn out the copies of *Plain Truth,* as do other presses in England and Australia. The magazine featured full-color photographs, coated paper, and imaginative design at first, but present format is modest.

Despite its current financial and legal troubles, the WCG continues to publish *Plain Truth* and to offer free subscriptions to its English, Dutch, French, German, and Spanish editions. Most of the articles relate to world news interpreted in relation to Armstrong's biblical prophecies. The October-November 1980 issue carried articles on race riots, the impact of television, world food production, the presidential campaign, the refugee crisis, and a review of *The Empire Strikes Back* movie.

The cover of the December 1979 issue carried a color photo of Pope John Paul II and President Carter. The lead article by Gene H. Hogberg, the magazine's news editor, purported to reveal the real reason for the Pope's visit to the U.S. At the UN, writes the WCG editor, the Pope "interspersed his carefully chosen words (he writes his own speeches) with patently Marxist egalitarian themes." Hogberg went on to report that in his various speeches in this country John Paul II often spoke about human values and the dignity of the human person, but that "the pope said nothing that I can recall . . . about the majesty of the almighty God, or the glory of the risen Jesus Christ who sits at His Father's right hand in heaven."

In the same issue, senior editor Jon Hill contributed a piece entitled "Ten Reasons Why I Don't Keep Christmas." Like Jehovah's Witnesses, the members of the WCG dismiss Christmas as a pagan festival that should be ignored by all genuine Christians.

Full-page ads in such national magazines as *Reader's Digest* and *TV Guide* invite readers to send in a coupon for a free subscription to *Plain Truth*. The cult's magazine carries no paid advertising; the substantial costs to print and send these free subscriptions are paid by members' tithes.

By 1971 the cult's programs were being carried by some 350 radio and 100 TV stations. Garner Ted Armstrong became a familiar TV personality to tens of millions of Americans, as well as to viewers in England, Canada, Spain, Portugal, South America, and Okinawa. Today the WCG message is heard on only about 50 radio and 60 TV stations in the U.S.

Ambassador College presses also churn out millions of copies of tracts, pamphlets, and books. Distribution centers for WCG literature have been set up in such places as Vancouver, Canada; Johannesburg, South Africa; Manila; Düsseldorf; and Geneva.

All WCG publications blast the New Morality, permissiveness, the drug culture, divorce, abortion, crime, and women's lib. They advocate patriotism, sobriety, thrift, chastity, and honesty. They play up natural disasters such as earthquakes, floods, and storms, as well as riots and wars, as biblically predicted preludes to the battle of Armageddon, which will usher in the utopian age of the "World Tomorrow."

The faithful expect Jesus to return to earth in the 1990s. His angels will conquer the armies of the world, and a resurrected David will rule as king over twelve great nations. Abraham, Isaac, and Jacob will help govern; Elijah will handle all religious and educational affairs. The races will be separated and will occupy different parts of the planet. (Armstrong traces many of the world's troubles to misguided efforts to integrate the races.)

For years Armstrong had groomed his son, Garner Ted Armstrong, to assume direction of the cult. Then, in October 1971, the 42-year-old son was removed as executive vice-president and vice-chancellor of Ambassador College. Garner Ted had received a doctorate in Child Psychology and Education from the College, where he also held the rank of professor of theology.

Later he was dropped from the WCG radio and TV programs, and ten-year-old tapes by the elder Armstrong were substituted. A subsequent issue of *Plain Truth* indicated that David Jon Hill had supplanted the younger Armstrong as managing editor.

A long explanatory letter from Herbert W. Armstrong, dated February 12, 1972, was read at meetings of the cult's congregations with instructions to destroy the letter immediately after the reading. The substance of the letter was that Dr. Garner Ted Armstrong was held "in the bonds of Satan." A *Time* magazine interviewer was told by the elder Armstrong that his son had confessed to an offense against "God, against his church and his apostle, against the wife God gave me in my youth, against all my closest friends."

Garner Ted Armstrong surfaced a few months later and resumed the radio and TV broadcasts. The nature of his "sin" was never spelled out, and he merely said that he had spent the time in a cabin in the Colorado mountains with his wife. His father announced to WCG congregations that now the church's work would take "the greatest lunge forward [it] has ever taken." He asked his followers to dig deeper to meet the church's financial needs and support the lunge.

A group of WCG ministers left the church in 1974 and set up their own Associated Churches of God. They accused WCG church leaders of living lavishly on the tithes of members and of covering up sexual offenses. Another group of dissidents, all graduates or former students at Ambassador College, started to publish a magazine that charged that Armstrong's teachings "have caused suicides, bankruptcies and hundreds of premature deaths. They have broken up thousands of happy marriages."

The Ambassador campus in England was closed, and in 1977 the campus in Big Sandy, Texas, was also shut down. Two of the church's three jet planes were sold. Armstrong made more frequent appeals to his remaining followers to contribute even beyond the required double tithe.

As schisms, defections, and financial problems rocked the Worldwide Church of God, the role of Stanley Rader took on more prominence. Longtime general counsel and treasurer of the church, Rader had not actually become a member until 1975, when he was baptized in a bathtub in Hong Kong by the elder Armstrong; he had been raised a Jew. During a *60 Minutes* televised interview with Mike Wallace in 1980, Rader confirmed that his annual salary exceeded

$200,000. Rader lives in a $300,000 Pasadena home and now receives about the same salary as the founder of the church. Before his excommunication, Garner Ted reported his own salary at $85,000.

Rader's former secretary married the octogenarian Armstrong, who was more than twice her age. Garner Ted has accused Rader of exercising a "Rasputin-like" influence over his father. The son says he has been unable to communicate with his father since the split. Rader's chances of succeeding the elder Armstrong improved when he was ordained a minister of the church (1979); previously he often noted that Jesus was a carpenter, not a priest.

When Garner Ted Armstrong was again disfellowshipped in 1978, he moved to Texas and began his own Church of God, International. His new headquarters were established in a simple red-brick building in Tyler, Texas, far from plush Pasadena. Two years later he reported that his new church enrolled about 3,000 members in 70 congregations, who contribute $1,400,000 a year; he was again being heard on about 50 radio stations. The elder Armstrong warned members of the WCG that they too risked excommunication if they offered any financial or moral support to his son.

At the end of 1978, Armstrong claimed that his WCG enrolled 100,000 members. Their tithes were bringing in more than $70 million a year to Pasadena headquarters. On Jan. 3, 1979, the State of California put the Worldwide Church of God into receivership; the basis for the action was a suit filed by six former members alleging financial misconduct. Court documents revealed that Armstrong spent $44,000 for a one-week stay in a Paris hotel and purchased $5,000 worth of Steuben crystal in Switzerland, using church funds. The suit said that Armstrong, Rader, and other church officials had siphoned off millions in church funds for their personal use.

Many organizations not allied with the Worldwide Church of God but concerned about the precedent being established by the action of the California attorney general, asked the Supreme Court to review the action. These included the National Council of Churches, the Catholic League for Religious and Civil Rights, and the American Civil Liberties Union. In a full-page advertisement in the *New York Times,* Armstrong said the attorney general "maintains that all churches are the wards of the political government—that the state owns all church property and assets and the political state should run and operate all churches." He added: "This is the most heinous and unconstitutional assault on American freedom, and start toward a communist dictator state." In late 1980, the California state legislature passed a law limiting the power of the attorney general to regulate the financial affairs of a church.

The attorney general, George Deukmejian, finally halted his investigation but complained that the legislature's action had handcuffed him, limiting his ability to prosecute cases involving alleged financial misconduct by church officials. The WCG was only one of a dozen churches once under investigation by his office.

The Worldwide Church of God launched a secular magazine called *Quest* in 1976. Armstrong hired Robert Shnayerson, once a senior editor at *Time* and editor-in-chief at *Harper's*, to edit the new magazine, which is dedicated to the "pursuit of excellence." The editor managed to assemble a first-rate staff; circulation climbed to 375,000 in less than four years. The WCG picked up annual losses of as much as $2 million — although both advertising and subscription revenues were growing.

In late 1980, Herbert W. Armstrong submitted an article on the Arab-Israeli crisis and on Egyptian President Anwar Sadat's proposed ecumenical center at the base of Mount Sinai. Editor Shnayerson rejected the article as not meeting the magazine's editorial standards. Nevertheless Armstrong bought a full-page ad in the *Wall Street Journal* to invite readers to study his article in the forthcoming issue of *Quest*. Shnayerson again refused to accept the article and appealed to Rader for support. When Rader refused to intervene, Shnayerson and his top five staff members resigned. Rader explained, "There is no such thing as the editor's autonomy. Mr. Shnayerson is not under any contract other than as a paid editor working under my control." Armstrong and Rader then began to seek a new editor more amenable to their wishes.

For several decades, Herbert Armstrong could point to a steady increase in church membership, larger and larger collections from tithes, a growing enrollment at WCG colleges, and a wider dissemination of his religious message. The unfavorable publicity, loss of ministers and members, schisms, legal actions, and especially the departure of the popular Garner Ted Armstrong may well foretell the end of the one, true church which began in 1933.

CHAPTER VI

Edgar Cayce and the A.R.E.

*Many study what America's most famous psychic
said in his sleep.*

Once a week in more than 1,500 homes around the country, groups of people meet to develop their spiritual powers and to study what Edgar Cayce said under hypnosis. During a period of 43 years, Cayce, America's most famous psychic, regularly put himself into a hypnotic trance and delivered a "reading." Transcriptions of Cayce's 14,000 readings provide the textbook and inspiration for these hundreds of study groups.

The groups are sponsored by the Association for Research and Enlightenment (A.R.E.), which has been chartered by the Commonwealth of Virginia to carry on psychic research. Membership in the A.R.E. is encouraged but not required for participation in a study group. Groups range from three to a dozen people and attract men and women from various religious backgrounds. For example, the A.R.E. group that meets Wednesday evenings in the home of Ernest O. Baxter, a Rochester, Indiana, druggist, includes three Methodists, a Presbyterian, two Disciples of Christ, two Spiritualists, and two Roman Catholics.

One of the 19 A.R.E. groups in the Minneapolis-Saint Paul area was formed by the wife of a Methodist minister. Many who have turned away from institutional religion, as well as church members, have joined A.R.E. groups, according to Mrs. Mary Trogen, head of the Bloomington, Minnesota, group. "People are looking for a more meaningful relationship to God and spiritual things and not finding it in the organized church," she says.

Cayce (pronounced *kay-see*) founded the Association in 1931. At his death in 1945, the organization reported only 700 active members. This number has grown to more than 17,000. In recent years, interest in the teachings of the sleeping prophet has grown steadily. Dr. Charles Thomas Cayce, a grandson, and a child psychologist by training, directs the work of the association in the U.S. and 15 other countries from headquarters in Virginia Beach, Virginia. All study groups follow the outline of lessons in the two-volume textbook by Cayce, *A Search for God*.

Each local group may conduct its meeting in its own way, but a typical meeting will include a period of meditation, Bible reading, and prayer, along with the study of Cayce's readings. Individual A.R.E. groups may also engage in dream interpretation, compare personal psychic experiences, and even try yoga and breathing exercises.

For more than four decades, Edgar Cayce practiced medical diagnosis by clairvoyance. He also elaborated a theory of reincarnation and the law of karma; described the civilization of the lost continent of Atlantis; and predicted such events as the destruction of New York City, Los Angeles, and San Francisco. Most of the words he spoke under hypnosis were taken down by his wife or secretary, and number at least 40,000 typed pages.

Thomas Sugrue's biography of Cayce, *There Is a River*, appeared in 1942 and catapulted the publicity-shy psychic into the national limelight. Some devotees say that Edgar Cayce's belief-system was somewhat colored by Sugrue's own background in Catholic mysticism. In any event, Sugrue's book, now titled *The Story of Edgar Cayce*, has seen 16 printings, with more than 500,000 copies in print.

More than a dozen other books, such as *Edgar Cayce: The Sleeping Prophet* by Jess Sterns, examine Cayce's readings on such subjects as ESP, health, reincarnation, and the like. These titles also find ready buyers.

Edgar Cayce was born on a farm near Hopkinsville, Kentucky, on March 18, 1877. As a youngster he reported conversing with his grandfather who had died some months before. He saw auras of colored lights around his friends and neighbors and assumed that everyone else saw auras too.

Years later Cayce reported a vision he had experienced at the age of seven or eight. While in a nearby woods, he had heard a humming sound and was startled by a bright white light. Then a figure clothed in white said, "Your prayers have been heard. What would you ask of me, that I may give it to you?" The lad answered, "Just that I may be helpful to others, especially to children who are ill, and that I may love my fellow man."

As a young man he joined the Disciples of Christ and began a career as a Sunday-school teacher, a lifelong avocation. Fundamentalist in his theology, Cayce read the Bible every day of his adult life and managed to read the entire Bible through every year.

His schooling ended at the age of 16. He wanted to become a preacher but had no money for college or seminary. At various times he worked on a farm, or sold shoes, insurance, and books.

His career as a salesman ended when he suddenly lost the use of his voice. A dozen doctors examined him over a period of ten months and prescribed treatment, but voicelessness continued; Cayce could speak only in a hoarse whisper. He was offered a job as a photographer's apprentice and quickly accepted, because he did not need to use his voice in the darkroom.

Discouraged by the medical doctors' lack of success in treating their son, Cayce's parents allowed a self-taught hypnotist to try his hand. The hypnotist, Al Layne, put Cayce into a deep sleep and suggested that he diagnose his own vocal trouble and prescribe a remedy. The sleeping patient replied: "Yes, we can see the body. The trouble we see is a partial paralysis of the vocal cords." Cayce awoke and found he could speak normally for the first time in nearly a year.

If Cayce could diagnose and cure himself, perhaps he could use his gift to help others. With Layne's encouragement, Cayce agreed to accept two patients a day for psychic diagnosis. The treatment recommended after the diagnosis covered a wide range of methods: osteopathic adjustments, drugs, diet, surgery, massage, poultices, herbs, yoga, and tonics.

On one occasion a distraught father brought his little girl to Cayce's office. She seemed to be choking to death, but X-rays had revealed no obstruction. Cayce quickly put himself into a trance and said that the child had swallowed a celluloid collar-button, which was lodged in her windpipe. The X-ray failed to detect the transparent button. The girl was rushed to a hospital, where the button was removed.

Eventually Cayce adopted a set pattern for giving his readings. He normally scheduled two a day, at 10 a.m. and 3 p.m. Cayce would take off his tie, open his collar, and unlace his shoes. He would lie on a couch or bed with his hands on his forehead. His wife or another associate would suggest that he go to sleep. Then the associate would give the name and the exact address of a person who sought diagnosis. Whether the patient was waiting in the next room or was hundreds of miles away made no difference. The sleeping man would give a diagnosis of the health problem and outline a treatment; many of these diagnoses were later verified by physicians. Someone copied down whatever Cayce said during the trances, and these transcripts comprise what are called the "readings." On occasion he would speak in fluent Italian or some other language, although while conscious Cayce knew only English.

Awake, Cayce knew nothing about medicine. He had never studied anatomy, physiology, pharmacology, or any of the health sciences. Yet when speaking in a trance, he gave amazingly accurate descriptions of the body. After prescribing certain spinal adjustments for a paralyzed man seeking his help from a town 300 miles away, Cayce gave these directions for supplementary treatment:

First, we would take eight ounces of distilled water. To this add garden sage one-half ounce, ambrosia leaves, not much stems, but leaves—one-quarter ounce. . . . Add Prickly ash and dog fennel, one-quarter ounce, and wild ginseng, one-half ounce. . . . Reduce this by simmering, not boiling too strong, to one-half the quantity. Strain, and while warm, add one and a half ounce 85 proof alcohol, with one dram of balsam of tolu cut in same. Then add three minims tincture of capsici. The dose would be half a teaspoonful four times each day, taken abot 15 to 20 minutes before meals.

Sometimes the ingredients he prescribed were hard to identify. During one reading he mentioned something called "clary water." No one knew what this could be; and Cayce, when awake, was no help. The anxious patient even put ads in several medical journals for any information about clary water. No one came forward with further information, so Cayce went into another trance and gave the formula for the mysterious ingredient. Shortly afterward a letter arrived from Paris, from a man who said his father had invented clary water but had not sold any for 50 years. The writer included the original prescription, which turned out to be identical to that dictated by Cayce while in a trance. Dozens of equally baffling stories are related by Cayce's biographers.

During his lifetime Edgar Cayce performed more than 9,000 psychic diagnoses. Sterns and other Cayce followers claim that he came close to 100 percent accuracy. Richard Woods, O.P., in *Occult Revolution: A Christian Meditation* (1971), commented: "His psychometric ability to diagnose illnesses was incredibly accurate; few errors have ever been found."

Cayce believed in prayer and meditation, but he was by no means a faith healer. He never disparaged the medical profession or advised clients to substitute faith for medicine. Cayce believed in the survival of the human soul, but he never consulted mediums or attended spiritualistic seances. He warned that those who studied his psychic phenomena should never be tempted to leave their own Christian churches: "No sect or schism should ever be allowed to form around this work." He also advised a follower to take this position concerning the readings: "If it makes you a better member of your church, then it's good; if it takes you away from your church, it's bad."

A chain-smoker himself, Cayce taught that moderate cigarette smoking would not harm the body. He also approved of drinking alcoholic beverages in moderation, though he thought that only wine actually fostered health.

Some of his health rules were drawn from folk medicine. One treatment he prescribed for a respiratory problem involved inhaling the fumes of apple brandy stored in a charred oak keg. He recommended eating three almonds a day to prevent cancer, and a weekly peanut-oil rub to ward off arthritis. Cayce urged people to avoid eating pork, but promoted the eating of fish, shellfish, fruits, and vegetables. His reducing diet was: eat all the apples you want and nothing else until you lose the desired weight. For thousands of American devotees, Cayce's rules of health carry far more authority than the advice of any medical doctor.

Cayce's readings took a new turn in 1923. Until then he had concerned himself only with health problems. Then, at the end of one of his psychic diagnoses, he added, ". . . in his last incarnation he was a monk." This was the first hint of reincarnation in any of Cayce's readings. At the urging of a wealthy printer from Dayton, Ohio, Cayce began to give "life readings," which purported to delve into individuals' prior lives.

When first told what he had said about reincarnation in his sleep, Cayce was horrified. The idea that the soul passed through many incarnations clashed with Cayce's traditional Protestant theology. Eventually, however, Cayce managed to harmonize reincarnation and his own religious convictions. He interpreted certain New Testament passages as proof of reincarnation (e.g., "Except a man be born again, he cannot see the kingdom of heaven")—and ignored those which denied his newly adopted belief.

Along with reincarnation, Cayce incorporated the law of karma into his beliefs. This law, or theory, which is anchored in Hindu and Buddhist thought, seeks to explain present misfortunes as punishment for misdeeds in some previous life. A man reaps what he sows—even though the harvest may come only in a new incarnation.

Until he incorporated the idea of reincarnation into his belief-system, Cayce held an orthodox Christian view of Jesus as the Son of God and the Second Person of the Trinity. Eventually he told his followers that in previous incarnations Jesus had lived as Adam, Enoch, Melchizedek, Joseph, Joshua, Jeshua, and others.

Astrology, too, overcame Cayce's original skepticism and took its place in the sleeping prophet's psychic theory. He accepted the influence of the planets, particularly at the moment of birth, but he considered astrology a flawed science because it ignores reincarnation.

In giving a life reading rather than a psychic diagnosis, Cayce would be told the individual's name, birth date, and place of birth. He would then speak of the person's prior incarnations in India, China, Egypt, medieval Europe, or colonial America. Cayce believed that he himself had once been a high priest in Egypt and a physician in Persia. Some of the incarnations he reported purportedly occurred in the submerged continents of Atlantis and Lemuria. Plato had first mentioned Atlantis 2,500 years ago; but most scientists doubt that such a technologically advanced society as that usually alleged for Atlantis ever existed.

Cayce believed that Atlantis had been a huge continent whose "life" extended from 10 million B.C. to 10,000 B.C., when it was inundated. A similar fate, he claimed, befell Lemuria in the Pacific Ocean.

Followers of Edgar Cayce maintain that he correctly foretold such events as the two World Wars and the 1929 stock-market crash. In August 1941, he predicted that World War II would end in 1945. In the same year, Cayce warned that New York City would be destroyed by earthquake or atomic attack by the year 2100. Before this catastrophe occurred, however, both San Francisco and Los Angeles would already have been wiped out. Much of Japan will someday (according to Cayce) slip into the ocean. Cayce also predicted that Russia would one day reject Communism and assume the spiritual leadership of the world, and that China would accept both democracy and Christianity.

A New York stockbroker, Morton Blumenthal, financed the opening of the 30-bed Cayce Hospital and Atlantic University in Virginia Beach. The school was intended to emphasize the study of the occult and parapsychology. But Blumenthal failed to heed Cayce's warning of pending financial collapse and lost heavily in the 1929 crash. Without his backing, the hospital and school closed. Today the A.R.E. headquarters is the former Cayce Hospital building.

Edgar Cayce never personally profited from his psychic abilities by picking growth stocks or winning race-horses or good spots to drill for oil—though he occasionally made attempts at such. He and his family lived modestly. He decided to charge $20 for a reading when the requests for such help began to take all of his time and energy.

The family had made several moves before settling in Virginia Beach. Since the town had no Disciples of Christ Church, Cayce joined the Presbyterian Church and continued his Sunday-school teaching. He lived across the street from Star of the Sea Catholic Church, and enjoyed long conversations with its pastor. Cayce read the daily newspaper and the Bible and little else. He never cultivated publicity or sought to demonstrate his gift on the stage. For recreation he liked to putter in his garden or go fishing.

During World War II, Cayce increased his psychic readings to as many as six a day; but the additional readings left him enervated. His son Hugh Lynn served with General Patton's tank forces in Germany, and his other son, Edgar, became an army captain. Cayce's health broke in 1944; he died on Jan. 3, 1945. To this day he remains one of the more baffling figures in American history.

The Association for Research and Enlightenment undertook the enormous task of cross-indexing the thousands of readings, which ran to about 12 million words. The A.R.E. defines a "reading" as "the term used to describe the clairvoyant discourses which Edgar Cayce gave while in a self-induced hypnotic sleep-state." Included in the Cayce files are 8,976 physical readings and 2,500 life readings (on reincarnation).

Hugh Lynn Cayce assumed the leadership of the A.R.E. after his father's death, but he made no claims that his own psychic powers came close to equaling his father's. He also admitted that Edgar Cayce was not very successful in "readings" designed to discover oil fields or buried treasure. Nor did a Cayce reading lead to the discovery of the whereabouts of the kidnapped Lindbergh baby.

In his writings and lectures, the son warned against dabbling in automatic writing, the ouija board, spiritualism, or drugs. A current A.R.E. leaflet states: "Experiments with ESP, telepathy, etc., are within the domain of trained parapsychologists, and have no place in the spiritual workshop. Such experimenting by the untrained, under uncontrolled conditions, can lead to many problems."

Even the harshest critics of Edgar Cayce admit that he was a simple, honest, God-fearing man. He seemed more amazed at what he said in his trances than anyone around him. During his lifetime, many people came to Virginia Beach, intending to debunk Cayce, and went away either disciples or simply baffled.

Sick people who followed the treatments given in a Cayce reading did get well. Perhaps many would have recovered their health anyway. Perhaps many were suffering from psycho-somatic illnesses. Perhaps the osteopathic adjustments and the diet and the herbs did the trick. But how did Edgar Cayce diagnose the specific ailment without knowing anything more than the patient's name and address?

Here is how Cayce himself explained his psychic powers: "Edgar Cayce's mind is amenable to suggestion, the same as all other subconscious minds; but in addition thereto it has the power to interpret to the objective mind of others what is acquired from the subconscious state of other individuals of the same kind. The subconscious mind forgets nothing. The conscious mind receives the impression from without and transfers all thought to the subconscious, where it remains even though the conscious be destroyed."

Anyone who accepts the possibility of extrasensory perception (ESP) can speculate that occasionally someone like Edgar Cayce will demonstrate this ability to a far greater degree than the average person could. Assuming the possibility of ESP, one can speculate that Cayce was "tuning in" on the thoughts of his patients or their physicians. Again, some evidence exists that Cayce possessed a photographic memory, and might have stored information on folk medicine and anatomy while working as a book-store clerk. Fundamentalist Protestants usually ascribe Cayce's feats to the work of demons. But many questions persist, and Edgar Cayce remains an enigma.

A typical Cayce enthusiast is Robert Figg, who teaches mathematics and computer programming, and who has been active in an Indianapolis A.R.E. group since 1966. Figg views the study groups as vehicles for developing spiritual powers. He himself is not an active churchgoer. Like most A.R.E. members, he keeps a book in which he records his dreams for later analysis. Dream interpretation forms part of the weekly agenda of his group.

Figg points out that A.R.E. members in the half-a-dozen Indianapolis groups often prefer physicians who are sympathetic to the Cayce treatments. Figg pays $35 a year to maintain his A.R.E. membership; for this he receives the Association's publications and has access to the readings and library at Virginia Beach.

Thousands of people visit the A.R.E. center in Virginia Beach each year. They attend free daily lectures and browse in a library specializing in books on parapsychology, dreams, reincarnation, ESP, and Atlantis. The Association sponsors workshops in various states, as well as a summer youth-camp.

Arnold Cluggish, another active A.R.E. member in Indianapolis, works for the treasury department and is a convert to Roman Catholicism. He sees no conflict between Cayce's teachings and those of the Church. Cluggish believes that there is some truth in all of the occult sciences—such as astrology, palmistry, and clairvoyance—but that these are merely "shortcuts" to spiritual growth and insight. He practices meditation 20 minutes each morning and evening, and says that meditation opens a "master gland" in the head that facilitates the flow of "spiritual energy."

"All the Christian churches have played down the value of meditation and missed many spiritual opportunities," says the pipe-smoking treasury agent.

Like most Cayce followers, he believes that the original Christian community accepted the idea of reincarnation, but that most references to this doctrine were removed in the Church's early years. "The church fathers accepted reincarnation," Cluggish maintains, "but thought it was best for the average man to believe he had only one life to lead." Cluggish believes that each person on earth is already in hell, that the soul between incarnations is in what we know as purgatory, and that the attainment of perfection, through a series of births and rebirths, is heaven. His A.R.E. group also includes Methodists, Baptists, and Presbyterians.

Participants in A.R.E. study groups are not required to sever connections with their own churches or accept all of Cayce's views on such questions as reincarnation and karma. Some people are mainly interested in Cayce's ideas on health. But despite the Christian creedal affirmation of the resurrection of the body, you will seldom find anyone long active in the A.R.E. who does not eventually accept the idea of reincarnation. As was mentioned earlier, Jesus himself is believed by many A.R.E. members to have appeared earlier in history as Joseph and Joshua; and some A.R.E. members identify Adam as Jesus in his first incarnation.

Thomas Sugrue put Cayce's philosophy in these terms: "The system of

CHAPTER VII

The Moonies

*Thousands of young Americans follow Rev. Moon
and his Unification Church.*

Africa and Asia are overgrown with hybrid cultic religions, derived from seeds planted by Christian missionaries but watered, pruned, and grafted by local religious entrepreneurs. These cults appropriate the name "Christian" and quote the Bible, but their creeds incorporate large chunks of magic, occultism, new revelations, astrology, sexual eccentricities, numerology, and folklore.

Rarely do these religions cross the oceans and gain much of a following in the U.S., although gurus, prophets, and swamis sometimes come to seek converts and financial support. Korea has been especially busy producing new semi-Christian cults—at least 60 by recent count—and one of these has managed to garner more than its share of headlines in American newspapers: the Holy Spirit Association for the Unification of World Christianity, which is the creation of the self-ordained Rev. Sun Myung Moon. It goes by the shorter name of Unification Church, and its adherents are popularly known as Moonies.

With only 7,000 fully committed Moonies in the U.S.—and perhaps three or four times that number of fellow travelers—the Unification Church might be regarded as only a speck on the religious panorama; but it has received far more attention and stirred up far more controversy than its present enrollment would seem to warrant. A dedicated Moonie works full time at his or her religion, and therein lies the reason for the attention the cult has attracted. These thousands of Moonies (almost all under 30) resemble full-time missionaries or evangelists rather than Sunday morning churchgoers. The hours and effort they put into propagating Unification beliefs give them an influence greater than that of the many-times larger number of "average" Christians. Rev. Moon clearly seeks to harness this energy—to change social structures, education, and politics, in the U.S. and throughout the world.

Tax-free income from the street-sale of peanuts, flowers, and incense by Moonies was estimated at $12 million during 1975 by the head of the American branch of the church. Some critics suggest that Rev. Moon receives under-the-table financing from the Korean CIA or Japanese industrialists; but there is a simpler reason for the church's increasing wealth. If only 1,000 young people net $50 a day apiece from begging or peddling, they will bring in more than $18 million in a year's time. Actually, far more than 1,000 Moonies engage in these fund-raising activities, and defectors report that $50 a day would be a very modest individual quota.

A new development in the cult's fund-raising has been the use of mobile fund-raising teams (MFT's). A team includes from five to eight members who leave their commune (each Moonie community is established as a commune) in a van and swoop down on a nearby community. Once the team reaches its destination, the MFT "works" Main Street or a shopping center, selling flowers, candy, and similar merchandise. A well organized MFT team can return $100 per person per day, to Unification headquarters.

The Unification Church recently bought the 42-story New Yorker Hotel in New York City for a reported $5 million. Members are refurbishing the 2,000-room building, which will serve as the cult's American headquarters, replacing former offices in the old Columbia University Club building purchased earlier for $1.2 million. The cult also owns the Manhattan Center (a former opera house) and the Tiffany Building, which houses offices for its national newspaper. The Moonies are said to be planning to acquire the Empire State Building. Their total U.S. assets in 1980 easily exceed $25 million—an impressive figure for a cult whose first missionary reached the West Coast in 1959.

Also in recent years, the Moonies have been buying property in Gloucester, Massachusetts, a predominantly Roman Catholic and ethnic-Italian city of 30,000. The mayor, city officials, and citizens have expressed dismay as the church continues to expand its holdings. One of its first properties acquired was International Seafoods, Inc., a lobster- and tuna-processing plant. The Moonies next bought a waterfront restaurant. They made an offer to buy a 30-room villa owned by a Connecticut-based order of Catholic nuns. The nuns refused to consider any offer from the Unification Church, but sold the property to a real estate broker for $1 million, who promptly resold it to the Moonies for $1.1 million. The new owners plan to turn the villa into a "professional education center." Gloucester joins a list of U.S. cities that have seen the cult's money used to buy up local businesses: Kodiak, Alaska; Bayou La Batre, Alabama; and Norfolk, Virginia.

Rev. Moon lives with his second wife and eight of his nine children in a $625,000 mansion overlooking the Hudson River in Tarrytown, N.Y. His children attend exclusive private schools. At his disposal are several limousines and a 50-foot cabin cruiser, christened *New Hope*.

All Moonies turn over their possessions to the church and become fundraisers. The disparity between their hand-to-mouth existence and the lifestyle of Rev. Moon is explained by Moonie leaders: if Moon himself lived in poverty, he could never hope to influence people of wealth and power in the U.S.

A confidential training manual for Moonie leaders explains: "Christians think that the Messiah must be poor and miserable. He did not come for this. Messiah must be richest. Only He is qualified to have dominion over things, and unless the Messiah can have dominion over things neither God nor the Messiah can be happy."

A crowd of 35,000 attended the cult's "God Bless America Festival" at Yankee Stadium in 1976. A rain storm ruined most of the decorations, and the attendance fell short of Moon's expectations; but those who came waved small American flags, sang patriotic songs, and heard an hour-long sermon by Moon interpreted by Col. Bo Hi Pak. Gangs of toughs set off firecrackers and smoke bombs and attacked some of the Moonies after the rally.

Earlier the Moonies had staged an extravaganza in Madison Square Garden that drew about 25,000; but many of the curious left before the program was over.

The church claimed that as many as 200,000 participated in their Washington Monument rally (1976); the National Park Service estimated the attendance at 50,000. The audience sat through a program of Korean dances, popular music, a 37-minute Moon homily, and a massive fireworks display.

The Unification Church invites some of the top scientists and scholars in the world to attend annual International Conferences on the Unity of the Sciences. Nobel laureates, Christian theologians, and others have participated. The Unification Church pays all expenses and reaps public-relations advantages, but makes no efforts to influence the discussions.

A few years ago, Sen. Robert Dole sponsored a congressional hearing to look into charges that the Unification Church brainwashes young converts and turns them into psychological captives who slave for 12 hours a day in return for skimpy room and board, while Rev. Moon and his family live in luxury. During the hearing, some parents testified that their children had, as Moonies, become spiritual zombies; other parents, however, expressed satisfaction that their sons and daughters had left a life of drugs, alcohol, or promiscuity to find a purpose in life as Moonies. Other government agencies have been investigating the cult's alleged control of a Washington, D.C., bank, the church's tax-exempt status as a religious organization, and its possible misuse of immigration visas.

Thus it is that, despite its tiny U.S. membership—less than that of some individual Catholic parishes—the Moon organization gets more than its share of headlines, magazine articles, and TV coverage.

Where did Rev. Moon come from? What does he teach? Is the Unification Church a Christian church?

Sun Myung Moon was born in what is now North Korea on Jan. 6, 1920. His family joined the Presbyterian Church when he was 10. At the age of 16, he said he was visited by Jesus on a mountainside and given a new revelation. Later he claimed that such personages as Moses, Noah, and Abraham had confided in him. These revelations were later compiled in a 536-page book entitled *Divine Principle*; the compilation was the work of an associate, Hye Won Yoo, who had earlier invented an air gun that launched Moon's business career. (Hye Won Yoo died in 1970.)

The Introduction to *Divine Principle* states that its purpose is to set forth the "new, ultimate, final truth." The book declares: "With the fulness of time, God has sent His messenger to resolve the fundamental questions of life and the universe. His name is Sun Myung Moon" (p. 16). The book holds the same position in the Unification Church that *The Book of Mormon* holds in Mormonism or *Science and Health* in Christian Science.

During World War II, Moon studied engineering at Waseda University, in Tokyo. He returned to North Korea and associated with a Pentecostal group that believed Korea would be the birthplace of a new messiah. Moon's teaching of that doctrine was considered heretical by the Korean Presbyterian Church, which excommunicated him in 1948. He then ran afoul of the Communist government and was twice sentenced to prison. United Nations forces freed Moon in 1950, and four years later he formally organized his new religion.

Moon divorced his first wife because, he said, she did not understand his mission. He remarried in 1960. His second wife was a high school teenager. (Some Korean critics of the movement say Moon has been married four times rather than twice, but this allegation is unproved. Also debatable is the reliability of accounts of ritual sex in the infant Unification Church.)

Moon not only started his own church, but he began to put together an industrial conglomerate in South Korea; it reported assets of $30 million in 1980. His various businesses manufacture air rifles, pharmaceuticals, ginseng tea, and titanium. Most of the workers in Moon's factories also belong to his church and accept below-normal wages to further the cause.

The South Korean government, which has harassed Catholic and Protestant churches, at first smiled on Rev. Moon's group. Moon's militant anti-Communism persuaded the civil authorities to let him conduct indoctrination programs for troops, and to provide him extra protection at his rallies. Moon denies that the late South Korean dictator Park Chung Hee (d. 1980) had shown him any favors.

Moon said that Jesus again appeared to him on Jan. 1, 1972, and told him to move to America. According to Moon's own account he replied: "I am a Korean man. I don't even speak the English language—how can I bring this message to America?" Jesus assured him: "I will open your way, and give you strength—America must hear these words before it is too late."

Moon immediately embarked on a mildly successful coast-to-coast preaching tour of the U.S. A few centers had already been established by Unification Church missionaries on the West coast. The church purchased a former Christian Brothers house of studies in Barrytown, N.Y., for $1.2 million. This Unification seminary, 90 miles from New York City, accommodates about 300 students. Several Christian and Jewish faculty members augment the Unification staff. Plans are under way to open a Unification university on another 300-acre plot owned by the church.

That Rev. Moon was able to win any followers in this country is a wonder. Unable to speak English, he preaches through an interpreter. His sermons have been known to last for several hours: typically, by the end of a talk, all but the most dedicated have quietly left the hall.

His early converts called him "Master," but he now seems to prefer the term "Father." Father and Mrs. Moon are looked upon as the True Parents of all Moonies. This aspect has upset many natural parents whose children have joined the cult. Moonie spokesmen say it should be no more disturbing than the practice among Catholics of referring to the pope as the Holy Father.

During the Watergate scandal (1973-74), the Moonies orchestrated a "God Loves Richard M. Nixon" campaign. Moon sponsored an ad published in newspapers across the country on Nov. 30, 1973, which, under the headline "Forgive, Love, Unite," urged support for the beleaguered President. The copy stated: "God has chosen Richard Nixon to be President. . . . Therefore, God has power and authority to dismiss him." The Moonies remained one of the few bands of loyalists during that painful episode and showed their support for the President by marching in front of the White House with pro-Nixon signs and sandwich boards. Moon himself met privately with the President during this period.

Moon sees the U.S. as the great bulwark against Communism and as the leader of God's forces in the coming holy war against the Soviet Union and China. His two most admired Americans are George Washington and Martin Luther King, Jr.

For most Moonies, their first introduction to the cult has been through a study club or discussion group on a college campus. Only later have they discovered that the group was sponsored by the Unification Church. Those who attend an introductory lecture on *Divine Principle* may be invited to come to a weekend retreat at a Unification center. The weekend's agenda consists of rounds of lectures, singing, games, and the like, with the objective of winning a commitment to the cult from the participants. Perhaps half of those who finish a weekend program affiliate with the movement.

Susan Reinbold, a public relations spokesperson for the church, estimates that about 35 percent of active Moonies come from Roman Catholic, 45 percent from Protestant, and 5 to 7 percent from Jewish backgrounds. Dr. Moses Durst, head of the U.S. branch of the church, was raised a Jew.

Full-fledged Moonies live in the 120 or so communes located around the country. They sleep only five or six hours a night, but are expected to work from 8 a.m. to 8 p.m. seeking converts or selling merchandise at a 400 percent markup. In shopping malls and airport terminals, when asked, they sometimes say that contributions go to (unspecified) programs for drug addicts or orphans; but Moon has excused these tactics as "heavenly deceit." All Moonies must agree to give up drugs, tobacco, alcohol, loafing, and sex outside of marriage. For their dawn-to-dusk efforts, they get a place to sleep, a barely adequate diet, and the opportunity to further the Kingdom of God in ways described in *Divine Principle*.

Mastery of the ideas in *Divine Principle* is the goal of every Moonie, but initiates of the cult also study such texts as *The Master Speaks, The Divine Principle and Its Applications, The 120-Day Training Manual,* and the *New Hope News* newsletter. *Divine Principle,* in its revised 1973 edition, is readily available to outsiders; but the other publications are circulated only among members.

Prof. Frederick Sontag, professor of philosophy at Pomona College and author of *Sun Myung Moon and the Unification Church* (1977), estimates a worldwide "firm" membership of 500,000, with another 2 million sympathizers. Several hundred thousand of the active members are in South Korea and Japan. Sontag calls the Japanese branch "the key to the financial growth and success of the worldwide Unification movement as well as the origin of the lifestyle." Total European membership is about 20,000, of whom 6,000 live in West Germany.

Rabbi Maurice Davis of White Plains, N.Y., a leader of an anti-Moon campaign, has compared the Moonies to the Hitler Youth of the 1930s. He says that the Unification Church tries to reach young people at a crisis point in their lives: after a broken romance, during an identity crisis or depression, in a time of loneliness. Potential converts are isolated in a strange environment at the weekend retreats, subjected to intense peer pressure, told that any turning back is the work of Satan, and urged to cut ties with family, friends, and former churches or synagogues.

Rabbi Davis maintains that the five characteristics of the Moonies are "a totally monolithic point of view, a fanatical following, unlimited funds, hatred of everyone on the outside, and suspicion of parents."

The Unification Church sometimes hides its identity through some 40 "front" organizations. Participants may not discover for months that Rev. Moon and the Moonies sponsor such groups as the One World Crusade, the Creative Community Project, or the International Federation for Victory over Communism. One front organization, called Judaism: In Service to the World, courts the Jewish community. Particularly successful enterprises have been the Korean Folk Ballet and the Little Angels of Korea. Once inquirers show interest, they find a group of new, clean-cut friends who tap their idealism, patriotism, desire for spiritual discipline, interest in peace or ecology, and impatience with the progress of their own churches or synagogues.

Working through a front organization called the Collegiate Association for the Research of Principles (CARP), the Moonies have intensified their missionary efforts on U.S. college campuses since 1979. As early as 1974, the Moonie newsletter, *New Hope News,* emphasized the importance of penetrating academia: "Father [Rev. Moon] said the college campuses are a major battlefield, and if we win there we will definitely win America" (May 10, 1974).

The first CARP chapter was founded in 1973 at Columbia University, but the growth of the movement was slow. The cult arranged a tour of 20 campuses in 1979. The Moonie caravan included 20 dancers from the church's International Folk Ballet, a rock group, and a number of speakers. Cult officials hoped to see 100 chapters operating by the fall of 1980.

CARP recruiters downplay any connection with the Unification Church. A brochure outlines the goals of the college-based affiliate as: "to seek harmonious and functional integration of religion and science; to promote cultural exchange of East and West; to formulate a new system of universal ethics; to offer critique and counterproposal to atheistic Marxist-Leninism; and to evaluate systems of higher education so that it may contribute in the development of the whole person."

Another Moonie influence on American campuses is the presence of the more than 50 graduates of the Unification seminary enrolled at various graduate and divinity schools. For example, eight Moonies have enrolled in the Harvard Divinity School, and others are attending Yale.

Moon's theological novelties lead most Catholic and Protestant theologians to deny that the Unification Church can even be called Christian. Certainly *Divine Principle* occupies ground far from that of mainline Christianity. A parallel might be found in the Mormon Church, which, like the Unification Church, accepts a new revelation in addition to the Bible (the Book of Mormon), a latter-day prophet (Joseph Smith, Jr.), and an assortment of beliefs unknown to the vast majority of Christians (secret temple rites, baptism for the dead, polygamy, and the like).

To Rev. Moon, the Bible is written in code, and he is God's chief cryptographer. Jesus himself imparted this secret knowledge to Moon in a series of visitations. As Moon writes: "There is so much to know, so many hidden truths within the Bible which are not written explicitly. If I revealed some of those secrets I am sure you would be amazed" (*A Prophet Speaks Today*, p. 138).

Basic to Moon's interpretation of the Bible is the idea of the three Adams. The first Adam was supposed to marry Eve and become the father of the perfect human family. Instead the serpent (Satan) seduced Eve. Moon claims that Genesis' reference to eating of the tree of knowledge of good and evil means to have illicit sex relations. Eve thought she could remove the stigma of her offense by having sexual intercourse with Adam without waiting to get God's approval. As a result, both Adam and Eve were driven out of the Garden of Eden and the original divine plan was frustrated.

Mankind had to pay a price, an indemnity, before God would send another Adam. Jesus, the second Adam in Moon's theology, was supposed to marry and beget perfect children. Jesus was a perfect man with a messianic mission but no more: "*Divine Principle* rejects the notion that Jesus was God Himself" (*Unification Theology and Christian Thought*, by Young Oon Kim, p. 130).

For some mysterious reason, Jesus did not marry, as young Jewish men in that age were expected to. The Moonies believe that John the Baptist failed to give Jesus his wholehearted endorsement, and thus became the chief villain in the thwarting of the divine plan some 2,000 years ago. The Jews rejected the Messiah, and the crucifixion of Jesus aborted God's second attempt to start a perfect human family. Jesus succeeded in winning spiritual salvation for humankind but failed in the equally important role of achieving physical salvation, the building of a Kingdom of God on earth.

The idea that God grieves is a basic Moon doctrine. "The center of Unification theology is to alleviate God's sorrow and to fill His heart with happiness" (Kim, p. 35). Both the first and second Adams were disappointments.

A third Adam must marry and start the long-delayed perfect human family that will usher in the kingdom. According to *Divine Principle*, the third Adam, or Messiah, will have been born in Korea between 1917 and 1930, will have married in 1960, and will live in America. As it happens, Moon was born in 1920, married for a second time in 1960, and now lives in Tarrytown, N.Y. He makes no public claims that he is the awaited Messiah, but understandably many of his followers make that assumption.

The public announcement of the identity of the Lord of the Second Advent is expected in the early 1980s.

Unification Church teaches that we live in the latter days; and that just as the

Jews in the days of Jesus rejected his claim to be the Messiah, so Christians in the 1980s will refuse to accept the third Adam.

A Declaration of Unification Theological Affirmation, adopted in 1976, states: "Christ will come as before, as a man in the flesh, and he will establish a family through marriage to his Bride, a woman in the flesh, and they will become the True Parents of all mankind. Through our accepting the True Parents (the Second Coming of Christ), obeying them and following them, our original sin will be eliminated and we will eventually become perfect. True families fulfilling God's ideal will be begun, and the Kingdom of God will be established both on earth and in heaven. That day is now at hand."

Moonism combines bits and pieces of occultism, spiritualism, astrology, shamanism, Christianity, Taoism, and numerology. It denies the Trinity, the divinity of Jesus, and his resurrection. Baptism and the Lord's Supper are identified with the failed mission of Jesus and are not practiced by the Unification Church. The cult's worship service consists of lectures, singing, and praying, with a minimum of ritual and no ordained ministers or sacraments.

Moon and the church hierarchy arrange marriages among Moonies. No Moonie can contemplate marriage until he or she has served the church for at least three years and has won three converts to the movement. When those conditions have been met, the young Moonie is believed to have reached the stage of conditional perfection. Dating and romantic attachments are forbidden. Qualified men and women members submit lists of five prospective mates. Church leaders arrange the matches, with Moon giving final approval.

Mass marriages have become a feature of the sect. Moon presided over the marriage of 1,800 couples from 25 nations in Seoul in 1975. Among the newlyweds were 70 American couples. The church forbids sexual relations for newly married couples for 40 days after the vows. The Unification Church does not recognize marriages contracted before joining the cult.

Moon teaches that all persons, living and dead, must be matched to achieve salvation. This even includes "Jesus," who has been paired off with a young woman now living in Korea.

In a ceremony at the cult's New Yorker Hotel headquarters in 1979, Rev. Moon matched (engaged) 700 couples, many of whom had never previously met their new partners. After the engagement ceremony, Moon administered "holy wine" to the couples. At the first pairing in Korea in 1960, several drops of Moon's blood were mixed with this wine. The original wine has been used for subsequent pairings, although replenished by adding new wine to the old. A mass marriage of up to 8,000 couples from around the world is being planned for 1981.

Parents are naturally dismayed when their children, bright students, suddenly drop out of college, begin peddling peanuts for 12 hours a day, and reject family and friends. Some frantic parents have hired professionals who kidnap cult members and try to get them to recant during marathon deprogramming sessions. The best known deprogrammer is Ted Patrick, a black man who once worked on Ronald Reagan's staff and says he has deprogrammed 1,000 cultists since 1971. Patrick accepts assignments from parents whose children have become involved with the Moonies, Hare Krishna, Children of God, Divine Light, and other cults.

Those who defend deprogramming believe it is the only way young people can undo the effects of the cult's brainwashing. But the Unification Church defines deprogramming as a "farcical term applied to the brute force used by mercenary inquisitors to break Church members' spirits and compel public recantation of belief."

Deprogramming involves three steps. First the deprogrammer has to get the individual into his custody. Sometimes the family will set up a ruse, such as an invitation to dinner; sometimes the deprogrammers kidnap the subject on the street and shove him or her into a waiting two-door sedan. Next the deprogrammer and his aides take the subject to a designated spot, usually a motel room. Third, the deprogrammer subjects the cult member to intense and often lengthy "counter-brainwashing."

This secular exorcism can last several hours or even days. In a motel room, guards stand at the doors; the windows are nailed shut. The deprogrammer seeks to bring the subject to the breaking-point by stressing the cult's doctrinal inconsistencies, by contrasting the lifestyle of the leaders with that of the rank and file, and so forth. Unification officials say about 400 Moonies have been deprogrammed and slightly more than half have returned to the cult.

Clearly the practice of deprogramming raises questions about the civil rights of the cult's members. If the Moonie is an adult—18 or older—his or her religious commitment may dishearten the parents, but this reaction alone does not give them legal or moral right to employ kidnappers or forced deprogramming. One person's intense religious experience may be another person's brainwashing. Jews have paid deprogrammers to win back children who accepted Christianity, and some Protestant parents have done the same to sever their children's allegiance to certain fundamentalist Christian sects.

If an adult son or daughter chooses a spouse whom the parents dislike, the law would hardly countenance a kidnapping and forcible detention to force the child to change marriage partners. Throughout history, parents have seen their children making choices in marriage, careers, religious faith, and politics with which they have disagreed. No parent wants a son or daughter to reject the family's religious and moral values. But this may be the price one has to pay for freedom of religion.

Patrick was sentenced to a year in jail and ordered to stop abducting cult members (1980). The superior court judge who pronounced the sentence said: "Punishment is needed to deter him and to protect the community. He will be a danger to society unless he changes his way of deprogramming. The forcible abduction of adults cannot be tolerated even under the guise of deprogramming or even if the parents want it done." Patrick had been convicted of kidnapping and conspiracy charges for the March 1980 abduction of a Tucson woman whose family said she belonged to a cult known as "The Wesley Thomas Family."

No one suggests that the Unification Church physically prevents members from leaving. But the Moonies and similar cults do seem to employ techniques that so weaken the will that the decisions of converts are suspect. Studies of Korean-war prisoners and of the personality change of Patty Hearst suggest that certain techniques can effect a dramatic change of belief and behavior. Some ex-Moonies maintain that these techniques have been used by the Unification Church with similar results.

The federal government hesitates to intrude into any religious dispute, but a sufficient number of parents have objected to the activities of the Unification Church to justify a congressional inquiry. The IRS is said to be investigating the income and expenses of the Unification Church, to see if it is still entitled to tax-exempt status. Critics contend that selling merchandise on city streets and turning over the proceeds to the Korean evangelist are not basically religious activities but a money-making scheme. The U.S. Immigration and Naturalization Service is looking at Rev. Moon's classification as a permanent U.S. resident and at the status of foreign Moonies in this country. The latter are here on tourist visas, not working visas, which would be required before they could legally engage in peddling. The Service judges that a sufficient number of U.S. citizens already qualify as peddlers, so the country does not have to import more.

A congressional subcommittee that studied the Unification Church reported: "Among the goals of the Moon organization is the establishment of a worldwide government in which the separation of church and state would be abolished and which would be governed by Moon and his followers." The subcommittee spent 18 months studying the cult in 1977 and 1978. The subcommittee's report included significant passages from a number of Moon's speeches and other statements: "The world is my goal and target. . . . Now when they are against us, then they are going to get the punishment. . . . Every people or every organization that goes against the Unification Church will gradually come down and die. Many people will die—those who go against our movement."

The report commented: "In the training and use of lower ranking members [the Unification Church] resembles a paramilitary organization, while in other respects it has the characteristics of a tightly disciplined international political party."

The subcommittee said it had found evidence that the Moon group had violated tax, immigration, banking, currency, and Foreign Agents Registrations laws, as well as state and local laws related to charity fraud.

Recently the Unification Church has taken the offensive against its many critics. It has filed a $4 million libel suit against the author and publisher of *Gods & Beasts: The Nazis and the Occult.* The complaint filed by the church's lawyers says that the book "falsely depicts" the Unification Church "as a fanatical occult group, and falsely compares it with the Nazi movement by ascribing to it elements similar to those which linked Germany's occult societies and the Nazi party." Other writers and publications have also been the targets of libel suits in recent years.

Although the government cannot judge Rev. Moon's theology, a growing number of Catholic and Protestant observers have leveled charges against the movement and its tactics. They point out that the Unification Church is the only "Christian" denomination depicting Jesus Christ as a failure rather than savior. According to Moon, Jesus botched his mission and let himself fall into the hands of his enemies. This set God's timetable back 2,000 years.

Moon has written: "God is now throwing Christianity away and is now establishing a new religion and this new religion is Unification Church." He predicts: "All the Christians in the world are destined to be absorbed by our movement." Other statements by Rev. Moon reveal his ambitions: "The time will come, without my seeking it, when my words will almost serve as law. If I ask a certain thing, it will be done. If I don't want something, it will not be done." He has told his followers, "I will conquer and subjugate the world. I am your brain."

Even though France reports only about 1,000 Moonies, one of the strongest criticisms of the cult from Catholic sources has come from the Archbishop of Paris, Cardinal François Marty. In a radio broadcast the cardinal said the Moonies "insinuate that they agree with the Catholic Church. This is false. They are dangerous, for they carry out indoctrination. They do not respect freedom. Let young people be very careful." In a later interview, Cardinal Marty asked: "Are we doing all that is necessary in our Christian communities to enable young people to meet Jesus? Rather than organizing a front against the Moon sect, let us examine our own consciences on this point."

Member churches of the National Council of Churches of Christ in the U.S.A. must declare their belief in Jesus Christ as Lord and Savior. This same affirmation is asked of Christian churches seeking to join the World Council of Churches. Would the Unification Church qualify for membership?

The NCCC commissioned a study of the theology of the Unification Church. Sister Agnes Cunningham, then president of the Catholic Theological Society of America, prepared the basic text of this study, assisted by several Protestant theologians.

Earlier the Moon church had tried to join the Council of Churches of the City of New York and had identified itself as "a Christian Church committed to the ministry of spreading by word and deed, the gospel of the Divine Lord and Savior, Jesus Christ." To test this assertion the study commission headed by Sister Agnes relied solely on the doctrines of the church outlined in *Divine Principle*. After careful study, the commission concluded that the Unification Church is not a Christian church. Specifically, its doctrine of the nature of the Triune God is incompatible with Christian faith, as is its Christology; and its teaching on salvation and the means of grace is inadequate and faulty as compared to orthodox Christian belief. The report was also critical of the emphasis in *Divine Principle* on the responsibility of the Jewish nation for the failure of the mission of Jesus. "The anti-semitism of *Divine Principle* is incompatible with authentic Christian teaching and practice," it declared.

What is clear from *Divine Principle* and other Unification Church texts is that the Unification Church represents an alternative to Christianity rather than a variation of Christianity. The fact that Jesus occupies a niche in Unification theology means little, for the same is true of many clearly non-Christian religions, such as Islam Bahaism, Spiritualism, and Theosophy.

American Jewish leaders are particularly critical of the Unification Church, both because of its alleged anti-Semitism, and because an unusually large proportion of Moonies come from Jewish backgrounds. "There are over 125 examples of an unremitting litany of anti-Jewish teachings in *Divine Principle*," charges A. James Rudin of the American Jewish Committee (*Science, Sin, and Scholarship*, p. 82). Rudin writes: "At a time when the majority of enlightened Christian leadership throughout the world is laboring to uproot the sources of the pathology of anti-Jewish hatred that culminated in the Nazi holocaust, Reverend Moon appears to be embarked on a contrary course of seeking to reinfect the spiritual bloodstream of mankind with his cancerous version of contempt for Jews and Judaism" (p. 75).

Why are numbers of young Americans joining the Unification Church, as well as the Hare Krishna movement, the Children of God, and scores of new and bizarre cults? J. Isamu Yamamoto says that most Moonies share one or more of the following characteristics: "They (1) are in search of an authority figure in their lives; (2) are alienated from their families and society; (3) have recently experienced an emotional trauma; (4) are attracted to an idealistic philosophy complete with absolutes; (5) have a background in a dead church that makes them vulnerable to and hungry for spiritual experiences; or (6) are newly converted to Christ and have had little or no biblical training and accept the doctrines of the Unification Church as true Christianity" (*The Puppet Master*, p. 50).

"Moon's Family offers the security of perennial childhood," writes Berkeley Rice in *Psychology Today* (January, 1976).

Some of the blame must be shouldered by a society that offers few standards of moral conduct and few goals to win the hearts of the young. For many young people, the sex-saturated, materialistic, drug-oriented culture they see around them has no appeal. The "straight" life of a new religion such as the Unification Church offers more hope. The promise to build the Kingdom of God on earth appeals to their idealism, and the friendship of others in the cult fulfills their desire for membership in community.

Harvey Cox, of the Harvard Divinity School, having studied the appeal of the Moonies and other new religions, wrote: "The real challenge is that Unification presents to idealistic young people a social vision aimed at peace, racial amity, ecological balance, and economic justice based on stories and symbols drawn directly from the biblical sources they have heard since they were young and from the American civil religion that still—despite Watergate, Viet Nam, and all the rest—maintains a grip on their imaginations" (*Christianity and Crisis*, Nov. 14, 1977).

Rev. Moon, on the other hand, warns that America is ill-equipped to confront a disciplined Communist society; that the lives of millions of Americans are characterized by moral flabbiness, hedonism, and the search for the perfect orgasm; that the sickness of family life is demonstrated by the growing divorce rate. When he invites concerned college students to leave such a society and help build the Kingdom of God, he finds many answering the call. Many people may well find more love and community in the Unification Church than they ever knew in their own families, churches, or schools.

Is Moonism a passing phenomenon? Professor Frederick Sontag visited Moonies in the U.S., Europe, and the Far East and became one of the few authors to interview Moon himself. Two of his major conclusions were that "the origins of the movement are genuinely humble, religious, and spiritual" and that "the adaptability and solidarity of the movement are such that we are dealing with a movement here to stay" (*Sun Myung Moon . . .*, p. 12).

Almost all American Moonies are under the age of 30, and the majority have been affiliated with the church for five years or less. Thousands join the church, stay for a few months or years, and leave. There exists no example, in a Western society, of a mature Unification Church embracing all age-groups.

Rev. Moon says he is making plans to establish self-supporting Unification cities and villages, which will be engaged in manufacturing and various businesses. The communal way of life now common among his young followers in the U.S. will then give way to family units. Begging and street peddling will no longer be necessary.

Actually the cult has experienced no membership growth in the U.S. since the mid-1970s. It has received a great deal of publicity, most of it unfavorable. Although Rev. Moon met privately with President Nixon, he has been ignored by Presidents Ford and Carter. Most members of Congress have become extra-sensitive to charges that they have been influenced by Moon (or any other South Koreans). Adverse actions by any of the various government agencies now investigating the cult may affect its future in the U.S. Any revelation, for instance, that the church has been used by South Korea's government to influence American policy might be devastating.

Deprogramming presents a moral dilemma. Children do grow up and make choices which their parents disapprove. But by age 18 they are adults in the eyes of the community and the law—free to make their own mistakes. All religious people should be concerned about the misuse of such legal devices as conservatorship to force people to denounce their religious beliefs. If the state can legitimately cooperate to force a young Moonie to leave a Unification commune, in principle it seems that it can also decide that a Trappist novice or a Salvation Army recruit should be returned to his or her family. Young people often do choose a life of sacrifice for spiritual motives, and that life may entail poverty, separation from parents, obedience to a religious superior, discipline, and hard work. A judge or jury is in no position to decide which causes are worth such sacrifices and which are not.

Yet such a choice should be freely made. The chief objection that many people have against the Unification Church is that it uses deception, manipulation, and brainwashing to recruit followers. To the extent that this charge can be verified, the choice of those who become members of the cult cannot be said to be freely made.

CHAPTER VIII

Scientology

L. Ron Hubbard abandoned science-fiction writing
to invent Dianetics and Scientology.

Hundreds of thousands of people have sought mental and physical health, a higher IQ, a better memory, stronger willpower, and a more attractive personality from the Church of Scientology. An outgrowth of the Dianetics fad of the early 1950s, this church identifies itself as an "applied religious philosophy" and a "spiritual technology."

The creator of both Dianetics and Scientology, L. Ron Hubbard has achieved a standard of living he could never have reached had he remained a science-fiction writer. One Scientology book suggests that Hubbard is "probably a millionaire several times over from his book royalties" and "probably today's highest paid writer" (*What Is Scientology?*, pp. 202-203).

Condemned by British authorities, ridiculed and scorned by medical and psychiatric societies, the Church of Scientology continues to win converts and establish new Orgs (local churches). The conviction of nine top Scientologists in 1979 on a charge of conspiracy to obstruct justice and the loss of a $2 million damage suit filed by a disgruntled ex-Scientologist rocked the church and brought unwanted publicity. But the church retains a large core of devotees and ample financial resources.

In the U.S., the cult is particularly active in southern California but also operates centers in major cities, such as New York, Washington, D.C., Chicago, Minneapolis, Seattle, Miami, and San Francisco. The church claimed a worldwide membership of 5,437,000 in 1977-78. It defines members as "persons with a current membership who usually but not always have enrolled upon a course of counseling or ministerial training." It asserts that 4 million people belong to its 38 U.S. congregations and 118 missions. This claim, if true, would make the Church of Scientology far larger than, say, the Episcopal Church (7,116 parishes) or the Churches of Christ (17,000 congregations).

No other church or sect has been quicker to pursue litigation to squelch criticism than the Church of Scientology. In 1974 it filed and lost a $2.5 million suit against the St. Louis *Post-Dispatch*, which had published a five-part series on the cult. The next year it filed a $5.6 million libel suit against the American Medical Association. The Minnesota branch of the cult filed a $1.9 million suit against the Minnesota Medical Society and the AMA. Other targets of Scientology libel suits (or threats of suits) have been ABC-TV, the Washington *Post*, the state department, the FBI, the CIA, the San Francisco *Chronicle*, Dell Publishing Co., and the Los Angeles *Times*. Church authorities also try to block publication and distribution of books critical of the movement. *What Is Scientology?* boasts that the Scientology churches in the U.S. "have succeeded in limiting and finally preventing publication of four such works." The same book relates the sad fate of individuals and organizations that have had the temerity to oppose Scientology.

L. Ron Hubbard holds the same position in Scientology as does Mary Baker Eddy in Christian Science or Joseph Smith, Jr., in Mormonism. Attitudes toward Hubbard run the gamut. Martin Gardner in his book *Fads and Fallacies in the Name of Science* (1957) observed: "To some he is an earnest, honest, sincere guy. To others he is the greatest con man of the century. Still others regard him as basically sincere, with just a touch of the charlatan, and now a tragic victim of his own psychoses" (p. 263).

He first won national attention in 1950, when he published *Dianetics: The Modern Science of Modern Health;* the book soon hit the bestseller lists and still sells a substantial number of copies in paperback. Combining elements of Freudian psychoanalysis and the Catholic confessional, Dianetics identified the "engram" as the "single source of aberrations and psychosomatic ills." These engrams are said to result from acute emotional shock or pain, and are recorded on the protoplasm of the cell itself. Dianetics taught that engrams could be recorded from the moment of conception; later, Scientology would explain that engrams could also be accumulated during previous lives.

Attempted abortions produced some of the worst engrams, but any traumatic event would leave its engram. These engrams could be erased if the patient were enabled to re-enact the event.

Hubbard wrote about two compartments of the mind: the analytic and the reactive. The analytic mind corresponds to the conscious mind; it is rational and, in fact, infallible. The reactive mind, however, stores up unpleasant memories (engrams). The purpose of auditing in Scientology is to bring these engrams to light and thereby eliminate them forever. As the engrams disappear over the course of the auditing, the analytic mind assumes complete control over the reactive mind—and the individual's troubles go away.

In his book, Hubbard claims that Dianetics "contains a therapeutic technique with which can be treated all inorganic mental ills and all organic psychosomatic ills, with assurance of complete cure in unselected cases" (p. 6). By driving out the engrams in the reactive mind, the subject's health will dramatically improve: "Discharge the content of this mind's bank and the arthritis vanishes, myopia gets better, heart illness decreases, asthma disappears, stomach functions properly, and the whole catalog of ills goes away and stays away" (p. 52).

A person who has ridden himself or herself of engrams is known as a "clear." Hubbard relates that the common cold has been found to be psycho-somatic. "Clears do not get colds" (p. 92).

Scientology evolved from Dianetics. It differs from Dianetics in that it introduced the concept of the *thetan* (or the individual consciousness, somewhat comparable to the "soul" in Christian terminology). Scientology also employs the "E-meter," a device used in auditing to identify areas of stress.

In the early 1950s, Hubbard set up the Hubbard Dianetic Research Foundation in Elizabeth, N.J. A few years later he transferred his headquarters to Los Angeles, to Wichita, and then to Phoenix. In 1954 he gave the movement a religious orientation and founded the first Church of Scientology in California. Critics claim that he came to that decision because he recognized the value of continuing his healing work under the protection of the First Amendment and with possible tax advantages.

In Scientology the newcomer is called a preclear. By confessing details of their past lives to an auditor (a minister of the Church of Scientology), preclears rid themselves of their "hangups" and thereby are enabled to develop their full potential.

During the auditing session, the preclear holds two tin cans that are attached to the E-meter. Should the preclear begin talking about an area of stress, the auditor will detect the stress by watching the movement of a needle on the E-meter. The auditor will continue to ask the same question until satisfied the truth has been told and the particular engram erased. Hubbard explains: "The E-meter is never wrong. It sees all; it knows all. It tells everything."

In the auditing process, the minister takes the subject back through his or her life, through the months before birth, and even through previous existences. The minister hunts for painful experiences or traumas that may have left engrams.

Psychoanalysis emphasizes the significance of early childhood experiences, but Hubbard attributes even greater importance to prenatal experiences. He insists that the embryo records engrams from violent sexual intercourse, masturbation, attempted abortion, and even from verbal abuse of the mother by the father. Hubbard minces no words in condemning abortion. "Anyone attempting an abortion is committing an act against the whole society and the future; any judge or doctor recommending an abortion should be instantly deprived of position and practice, whatever his 'reason.' " Even the most dedicated right-to-life advocate could hardly take a firmer stand against abortion.

Hubbard's anti-abortion position goes back to *Dianetics*, in which he wrote: "A society which suppresses sex as evil and which is so aberrated that any member of it will attempt an abortion is a society which is dooming itself to ever-rising insanity. For it is a scientific fact that abortion attempts are the most important factor in aberration. The child on whom the abortion is attempted is condemned to live with murderers whom he reactively knows to be murderers through all his weak and helpless youth!" (p. 132).

The fact that some Scientology preclears relate accounts of being raped by their fathers is easily explained in Dianetic theory. They understand the act of coitus between their parents as rape. Hubbard explains that a fetus as young as nine days after conception can receive an engram from parental intercourse.

A further teaching of Scientology is that the bodies inhabited by a particular thetan may not have been human bodies at all. The same thetan may have animated many different species, according to Scientology's theology. *Time* magazine gave Hubbard's explanation of why someone might have difficulty crying—"he was once a primordial clam whose water ducts had been clogged with sand" (April 5, 1976).

The E-meter played no part in the original formulation of Dianetics. Hubbard later adopted the use of the E-meter, as a short-cut to discovering engrams. Far less sophisticated than the polygraph-type lie detectors used by law-enforcement agencies, the E-meter simply attempts to measure changes in the electrical resistance on the surface of the skin. Hubbard has also reported using the E-meter to pick up subtle emanations from tomatoes as well as from people.

Scientologists are urged to buy their own E-meters, priced (in 1980) at $1,000 (regular model) or $2,000 (deluxe). To be on the safe side, the church suggests they also buy a spare E-meter for emergencies.

Although he lacked any medical training, Hubbard put full confidence in his discovery of Dianetics. As the preclear sheds engrams, he or she approaches the state of the "clear" or "optimum individual" who has no psychoses, neuroses, compulsions, or repressions. The clear can even expect to regain optimum eyesight and hearing.

The beauty of Dianetics was that it offered a single explanation for all types of disorders. Treatment supposedly costs less than psychoanalysis, and the auditors needed no lengthy medical training. Some Scientology auditors are still teenagers; the youngest on record was only 15. But the Church of Scientology claims that its teaching does not oppose medical science and that church policy requires applicants who are medically ill to consult with a competent physician before receiving Dianetic counseling.

People have probably been healed by every type of psychotherapy: psychoanalysis, Christian Science, yoga, New Thought, faith-healing, voodoo, and Dianetics. Auto-suggestion explains many of these results. No doubt men and women have also been helped by Scientology. But the question is: how many people have been hurt by Scientology?

After 160 days of hearing testimony, the Supreme Court of Victoria, Australia, declared, "Scientology is evil; its techniques evil; its practice a serious threat to the community, medically, morally, and socially; and its adherents are sadly deluded and often mentally ill." The court furthermore called the Church of Scientology the "world's largest organization of unqualified persons engaged in the practice of dangerous techniques which masquerade as mental therapy."

Subsequently, the Victoria parliament passed a law (1965) banning the teaching, application, or advertising of Scientology. But the law was repealed in 1973, and the Church of Scientology now has tax-exempt status as a religious sect in Australia.

A former British Minister of Health, Kenneth Robinson, has said that Scientologists "direct themselves to the weak, the unbalanced, the immature, the rootless, and the mentally and emotionally unstable." He added that their "authoritarian principles . . . are a potential menace . . . to the personality and well-being of those so deluded as to become its followers."

Although "Ron," as he is called in the cult's literature, formally withdrew as head of the movement in 1966, no one doubts that he still controls its direction. He has written all of the authorized Scientology texts, and he continues to issue executive memorandums to his followers.

Born in Tildon, Nebraska, in 1911, Lafayette Ronald Hubbard claims to have graduated from Columbian University, a division of George Washington University. Actually Hubbard dropped out of college after his sophomore year. He describes himself as an engineer, author, and philosopher. He used to sign his name with a Ph.D. from Sequoia University. Sequoia, formerly known as the College of Drugless Healing, had granted Hubbard an honorary doctorate for his discovery of Dianetics. He then began to use "D.Scn." (Doctor of Scientology) after his name.

Scientology biographies of the founder say he grew up on his grandfather's ranch in Montana but sometimes accompanied his father, a Navy officer, on tours of the Far East. He has claimed to have received secret wisdom from such diverse sources as an American Indian medicine man and a Tibetan monk.

Hubbard served as an officer in the U.S. Navy during World War II and began a career as a science-fiction writer after the war. In fact his first exposition of Dianetics appeared in the pages of the May 1950 issue of *Astounding Science Fiction*.

Hubbard claims he was twice declared medically dead, once for eight minutes. (Such a miraculous return to life is the familiar shaman's initiation and the source of supernatural powers.)

In 1949, lecturing to a group of fellow science-fiction writers, Hubbard mused: "Writing for a penny a word is ridiculous. If a man really wanted to make a million dollars, the best way would be to start his own religion."

Publication of his book *Dianetics* briefly illuminated the pop-psychology skies in the early 1950s. The book jacket called Dianetics "a milestone for man comparable to the discovery of fire and superior to the wheel and the arch."

In a few years most of the ideas of Dianetics reappeared as Scientology. Hubbard set up churches in California and in Washington, D.C., but left the U.S. in 1959 to settle in England. There he bought the mansion and its 57-acre estate which had been owned by the Maharajah of Jaipur: Saint Hill Manor in East Grinstead, Sussex. This is now international headquarters for the cult.

Hubbard and his third wife and some of his children live at Saint Hill Manor. When the British Ministry of Health stripped the College of Scientology of its status as an educational institution in 1968, Hubbard left England for a time and lived on a converted cattle-boat called the *Apollo*. This became the "flagship" of a small fleet known as the Sea Org, which visited various ports in the Mediterranean and along the African coast. Its ships were manned by about 300 Scientologists.

With its ships now in moth balls, Scientology retains the Sea Org as a sort of religious order within the church. Dedicated members may be invited to membership and sign billion-year contracts to serve the cause of Scientology.

The awe with which Scientologists view the Founder is illustrated by the following question-and-answer from *What Is Scientology?* (p. 202):

"Question: Does L. Ron Hubbard eat food, and sleep?

"Answer: Oh yes, he has a body, and bodies need food and sleep to run well. But at an age when most men have packed it up, Ron still outworks any of those around him. And sleeps less."

One John McMaster of South Africa became the first certified clear in the history of Scientology, in 1965. He has since broken with Hubbard and the church. Now the cult turns out 15 to 20 clears a week who complete the "advanced course" at Saint Hill Manor. About 20,000 people are now certified clears; they spend from $5,000 to $10,000 to achieve their clear status.

Clears are eligible to continue their Scientology training by working toward the eight Operating Thetan grades above Clear. The first two of these grades,

Operating Thetan I and II, were unveiled by Ron in 1966; and the most recent (VIII) was offered in 1978. The cult describes an Operating Thetan as "a spiritual being operating independently of the laws of the physical universe" (*What Is Scientology?*, p. 325). The cost of the Saint Hill Special Briefing Course was quoted as $16,537.50 — but the cost was expected to rise monthly because of inflation.

The authors of an unusually sympathetic book about Scientology explain: "As one proceeds further and further up the OT levels, one becomes more and more aware of himself as separate from the body. Some OT's even speak of the ability to go exterior from the body at will. And this state of exteriorization is to be understood as completely literal" (*The Truth about Scientology*, pp. 239-240).

L. Ron Hubbard has written dozens of books on Dianetics and Scientology; his first book alone has sold millions of copies. He still produces one or two books a year, which are eagerly snapped up by devotees. His books, tapes, movies, cassettes, photos, and busts fill Scientology Orgs. He receives royalties on all these books and materials. Each local Church of Scientology also sends 10 percent of all contributions for training and counseling to Saint Hill headquarters.

Hubbard seems to be one of the few people in the world who have found the answer to the problem of inflation. Citing the rising cost of printing and paper, he decreed in May 1979 that "beginning 1 June 1979 the price of all Dianetic and Scientology books and other materials including meters will increase at the rate of 10% per month, effective at midnight each month on the last day of the preceding month." This Executive Directive from "Ron" contains the notation: "LRH ED 284, THE SOLUTION TO INFLATION, Cancels LRH ED 284-1 and amends LRH ED 284-4."

A price increase of this magnitude means that a 74-page book (such as *Introduction to Scientology Ethics*) that sold for $6 on June 1, 1979, would cost $17.12 only a year later and in 24 months would carry a price tag of $53.70. And most Scientology books are more expensive: the *Technical Bulletins of Dianetics and Scientology*, in 10 volumes, sold for $544.50 in the fall of 1979. In a few years, only the wealthiest people in the U.S. could possibly afford to buy a Scientology text. Cultists are urged to buy the complete LRH Library. In September 1979, the entire set cost $1,607 — and this figure was going up 10 percent per month.

Converts start off in Scientology through a $30 introductory course which extends over five evenings. They soon discover that to reach the first plateau costs about $650 for a 12-hour "Life Repair" course. The average person spends $5,000 or more to reach "clear" status. Some disenchanted people who have left the cult report they were urged to sell their automobiles and possessions to pay for their auditing. Some Scientologists become auditors themselves in order to work off their own debts acquired in auditing. Anyone who goes all the way to Operating Thetan VIII has invested something like $15,000 in courses, auditing, books, and travel.

All visitors to a local Org must reveal their names and addresses. Newspaper reporters and other investigators are not welcome. They are likely to be categorized as suppressives, that is, people who wish to harm the growth and progress of Scientology. Since devout Scientologists view the cult as the one sure path to a world without war, crime, or mental illness, they hold strong negative feelings about the slightest criticism.

A 1967 policy letter from Ron identified suppressive persons as "fair game" who may be "tricked, sued, lied to, or destroyed." This memorandum has since been retracted. *What Is Scientology?* explains, however, that "when such a person [a suppressive] exists in an area, a trained Scientologist applies special technology used in detecting and handling him so as to protect himself and others from harm" (p. xxvi). The cult has recently been charged with harassment of its critics; the temptation for overzealous Scientologists to stop even objective investigations of the movement is obvious.

Although the creed of Scientology affirms "that all men have inalienable rights to think freely, to talk freely, to write freely their own opinions and to counter or utter or write upon the opinions of others," the actions of the cult in initiating libel suits and threatening litigation belie the creed. Hubbard's Code of Honor, which appears in many Scientology publications, includes point 12: "Never fear to hurt another in a just cause."

Preclears find themselves engaged in a variety of drills. In one such session the auditor confronts the preclear with a series of questions similar to those typically posed by a Zen master. In another the preclear participates in an "Alice in Wonderland" dialogue based on disconnected phrases from the Lewis Carroll story. Instructions for still another training session tell the preclear to stare at another person for ten-minute stretches without any movement, twitching, or even blinking. In "bull baiting" drills, the instructor attempts to get a reaction by insulting the preclear with vulgar attacks on his or her physical appearance, sexual prowess, intelligence, and so forth.

Special efforts have been made to enroll celebrities in the cult. The cult operates so-called Celebrity Centers in Los Angeles, Las Vegas, New York, and Toronto. Past or present Scientologists include actor Stephen Boyd, former football star John Brodie, the late Mama Cass Elliot, Karen Black, Priscilla Presley, and John Travolta.

Dianetics made no claim to a theological base. Yet Scientology needed such a base to qualify as a religious organization. Hubbard consequently revealed that each person has a thetan that roughly corresponds to the Christian idea of the soul. This thetan has existed for billions, if not trillions, of years, inhabiting one body after another and picking up engrams as a ship collects barnacles. Hubbard once speculated that the age of the average thetan is about 74 trillion years.

Reincarnation has, of course, become a basic part of Scientology theology. "It is a fact that unless one begins to handle aberrations built up in past lives, he doesn't progress satisfactorily" (*What Is Scientology?*, p. 201). With an accumulation of engrams over billions and trillions of years, it is a wonder anyone achieves "clear" status.

During a christening, the Scientology minister introduces the thetan to its new body as well as to the parents and godparents. The minister then thanks the thetan for its participation.

Since Scientology assumed religious garb, it has developed ceremonies for worship, marriages, funerals, and other religious occasions. The church observes two major holidays: Ron's birthday (March 13) and the anniversary of the date of the publication of *Dianetics* (May 9).

Although Scientology is obviously incompatible with Christianity, the cult states: "Membership in Scientology does not mean that there is any necessity to leave your church, synagogue, temple, or mosque" (p. 201).

In 1967, Hubbard wrote: "Scientology does not conflict with other religions or religious practices as it clarifies them and brings understanding of the spiritual nature of man. Scientology has among its members people of all major faiths, including many priests, bishops, and other ordained communicants of the major faiths." It would be difficult to imagine a Catholic priest in good standing, much less a bishop, who would affiliate with Scientology. The cult capitalizes on any Hollywood celebrities who take up Scientology, but it has yet to identify any Catholic priest who has tried to maintain a dual membership in the Church of Rome and the Church of Scientology.

In a recent year, the cult claimed an ordained ministry of 5,950 men and women who serve some 79 churches and 172 missions around the world. Scientology statisticians say about 60 percent of church members are in their 20s. They report that 26 percent come from Roman Catholic, 41 percent from Protestant, and 7 percent from Jewish backgrounds.

The U.S. government hesitates to deny religious status to any group describing itself as religious. England, however, still refuses to grant the Church of Scientology such status. English authorities removed the College of Scientology from the list of approved educational establishments. Technically this means that foreigners may not enter the country to study Scientology at Saint Hill Manor. In practice, many non-English Scientologists do go to the headquarters to achieve clear status or the higher degrees of the cult.

Libel suits and threats of litigation against critics were apparently not sufficient measures of "self defense" for the Scientology hierarchy. On June 11, 1976, two Scientologists were discovered inside the U.S. courthouse in Washington, D.C., with forged Internal Revenue Service credentials. One entered a guilty plea and received a sentence of two-years probation. The other, Michael J. Meisner, fled to the West Coast but surrendered to authorities a year later. He told the FBI that Scientology officials in Los Angeles urged him to stay in hiding, that when he showed signs of wavering he was put under "house arrest," gagged and handcuffed, but that he managed to escape.

Meisner told a story of extensive covert operations carried out by top Scientologists since 1975. Church spies had infiltrated the IRS, the Drug Enforcement Administration, and the tax division of the Department of Justice. Scientologists, he said, stole documents that they copied and returned. He related that Scientologists had bugged an IRS conference room in Los Angeles to try to learn the actions being planned against the church.

Relying on Meisner's confession, the FBI organized a 100-person raid on Scientology headquarters in Los Angeles and Washington on July 8, 1977. They carried away thousands of documents, a blackjack, two pistols, ammunition, a lock-picking kit, knockout drops, and bugging equipment. The haul included CIA documents marked "secret."

Documents seized in the massive raid also revealed that the Church of Scientology had systematically identified, attacked, and attempted to discredit its critics. A folder labeled "Operation Freakout" contained a detailed scheme to "incarcerate Paulette Cooper," a free-lance writer and critic of the cult.

Nine members of the church, including Mary Sue Hubbard, the founder's wife, were convicted in October 1979 for participating in conspiracy to steal government documents. Most received sentences of four to five years in prison and $10,000 fines. Two other top-ranking Scientologists were sentenced in 1980 to terms of two to six years for what prosecutors called a conspiracy to infiltrate the Internal Revenue Service and the Justice Department in order to steal or copy documents. Jane Kember and her aide were extradited from England in late 1980, to stand trial in the U.S. Mrs. Kember was the third-ranking official in the Scientology hierarchy at the time of her extradition.

If all this was not enough trouble for the embattled church, there was more to come. A Portland, Oregon, jury awarded an ex-Scientologist more than $2 million in 1979 after the plaintiff charged that the Church of Scientology had defrauded her by promising to make her life better. Instead, said Mrs. Julie C. Titchbourne, 22, she spent $3,000 for various Scientology courses and suffered severe emotional distress while she was a member of the cult in 1975 and 1976. The jury agreed with her that the church had committed fraud and awarded her punitive damages of $1.9 million and compensatory damages of $153,000. The defendants were the Church of Scientology of Portland, the Scientology Mission of Davis in Portland, and the Delphian Foundation, an organization staffed by Scientologists.

Mrs. Titchbourne said she was told the courses would help her in her college studies, raise her IQ test scores, and improve her creativity. The Oregon Supreme Court had ruled that the case could be brought to trial by rejecting the Scientologist claim that the Church of Scientology was protected from such suits by the freedom-of-religion provisions of the federal and Oregon constitutions. The judge told the nine jurors that if Scientology's promises were of a religious nature, the church could appeal to such constitutional protection. The jury unanimously arrived at the verdict of fraud. A church statement attacked the verdict and said, "This decision is a blow to all of those who cherish the right to practice their religion free from the harassment of psychiatrists and de-programmers who have appointed themselves self-styled inquisitors."

Documents seized in the 1977 FBI raid also confirmed that the Church of Scientology planned to gain control of city government and the news media in Clearwater, Florida. When the mayor of this Gulf Coast resort city, Gabriel Cazares, opposed the purchase of two downtown buildings for $3 million in cash by a group called the United Churches of Florida, he was made the target of a Scientology-directed smear campaign. The United Churches turned out to be a front for the Church of Scientology. Scientologists faked a hit-and-run accident by a car in which Cazares was a passenger, in an attempt to discredit him in his campaign to win election to Congress.

As usual the church sought to silence any criticism. But when it filed a $1 million suit against the Clearwater *Sun*, the newspaper countersued for abuse of legal process and subpoenaed the church's financial records. The Scientologists dropped their suit. The St. Petersberg *Times* filed suit to enjoin the Scientologists from harassing its reporters and published a 14-part series on the cult. Two reporters for this newspaper received the 1980 Pulitzer Prize for their series on Scientology.

Cazares' successor as mayor, Charles LeCher, has called the Church of Scientology more of a "secret society" than a religious organization. He told an anti-Scientology rally in 1979, "I'm going to keep working to get them out of Clearwater."

A former Scientologist filed a $200 million suit against the church in December 1979, charging it had cheated thousands of converts by subjecting them to "mind control." Lavenda Van Schaick said the church had persuaded her to divorce her husband, spend $13,000 on auditing, and work for the church without pay for nine years in Las Vegas and Clearwater.

In the latest in a long line of libel suits filed by the Church of Scientology, a federal judge in 1979 dismissed the church's claims that co-authors James Siegelman and Flo Conway had libeled Scientology in their book *Snapping: America's Epidemic of Sudden Personality Change* (1978). Judge Gerard L. Goettel examined 15 allegedly libelous statements by the authors and declared that the statements were all "clearly either nonlibelous or statements of opinion."

The Scientologists were particularly upset over the authors' discussion of the influence of Scientology on Charles Manson. They maintained that Manson learned many of the mind-control techniques he employed in his "Family" from his study of the Scientology cult while in prison.

Manson's attraction to Scientology and its role in his development have been described in considerable detail by Vincent Bugliosi and Curt Gentry in their book *Helter Skelter: The True Story of the Manson Murders* (1972). Bugliosi was the prosecuting attorney in the Manson trial for the murders of Sharon Tate and Leno and Rosemary La Bianca.

The authors of *Snapping* wrote: "The reports we have seen and heard in the course of our research, both in the media and in personal interviews with former Scientology higher-ups, are replete with allegations of psychological devastation, economic exploitation, and personal and legal harassment of former members and journalists who speak out against the cult" (p. 161). They concluded that Scientology led its devotees "to levels of increasingly realistic hallucination" (p. 163). Their assessment of the cult was that "the bizarre folklore of Scientology is a *tour de force* of science fiction. . . . More than anything else, this combination church and therapeutic service trains people in hallucination and delusion."

The judge granted that some of what the authors of *Snapping* said was "unflattering" but that "none of these statements go beyond what one would expect to find in a frank discussion of a controversial movement." After the verdict Siegelman and Conway issued this statement: "We hope this decision established the precedent that authors are not defenseless — at least as long as there are bold lawyers like [defense attorney Melvin L.] Wulf — and that neither authors nor publishers need to be helpless victims of any organization that may seek to suppress public discussion or the free expression of fact and opinion." A spokesman for the church denied the charge of legal harassment and said: "It has been a longstanding Church policy to use the courts only as a last resort."

Paulette Cooper filed a $20 million suit against the Church of Scientology of New York, charging the church with a "calculated and reckless plan" of harassment over a five-and-a-half-year period. In her complaint she said the records showed that she was the target of a campaign whose purpose was to "incarcerate Paulette Cooper in a mental institution or put her in jail." Her publisher withdrew her book, *Scandal of Scientology*, and destroyed most of the copies immediately after publication (1971) in the face of defamation suits totaling $15 million filed by various branches of the Church of Scientology.

Specifically Miss Cooper said that certain Scientologists, in December 1972, had stolen some of her personal stationery, used this to write a bomb-threat purportedly from her, mailed it to themselves, and then reported the bomb-threat to the FBI. Subsequently she was indicted for sending a bomb-threat through the mail and for committing perjury in denying the charge. The charges were eventually dismissed. Altogether the Church of Scientology instituted 14 law suits against Miss Cooper.

Although the activities and methods of the Church of Scientology have come under increasing attack in the media, the cult has found champions in several syndicated columnists, such as James J. Kilpatrick, Mary McGrory, and Nicholas Von Hoffman. Von Hoffman wrote: "Scientology, of course, makes as much or as little sense as 'Presbyterianism,' but since it's different and it hasn't been in business for 300 years, its members can be robbed of their First Amendment rights and no congressional investigations are convened."

Writing in the December 1968 issue of the American Medical Association's *Today's Health*, Ralph Lee Smith warned: "Before it finally goes the way of all cults, Scientology may leave behind a legacy of tragedy unmatched in the annals of fads and fallacies in mental health."

CHAPTER IX

Transcendental Meditation

*A technique to reduce stress for some,
a way of life for others.*

A large number of Americans start their day by finding a quiet spot, closing their eyes, and meditating for 15 or 20 minutes. Many follow the same routine before dinner. They spend this time in meditation in order to calm down, sweep out the mental cobwebs, lessen stress and tension, reduce blood pressure, and improve their memory or reasoning ability. They hope that regular practice of meditation may help them avoid a stroke or heart attack. Evidence suggests that such meditation works for most people most of the time.

By far the most popular method is that taught by the Indian guru Maharishi Mahesh Yogi: Transcendental Meditation (or simply TM). More than 600,000 Americans have paid the fee to take the TM course, and an estimated 30,000 people enroll every month. Dr. Herbert Benson of the Harvard Medical School wrote in his best-seller *The Relaxation Response* (1975) that TM works but that no one needs to pay the $125 initiation fee or receive a secret mantra to get the same benefits.

It is fairly obvious that a few minutes set aside during a hectic working day will improve almost anyone's mental and physical state. Some Christians wonder, however, whether the Maharishi's own Hindu orientation, the secret mantra, and the cult's quasi-mystical initiation ceremony give TM a religious character in conflict with the Gospel.

Certainly the current interest in meditation in the U.S. can be attributed to the Maharishi, perhaps the most successful of the roster of gurus, swamis, yogis, and assorted wise and holy men who have tried to carry Eastern philosophies to the West. Born in the Kahatriya (or warrior) caste, in 1918, he received a degree in physics in 1942 from Allahabad University. Instead of pursuing a career in science or business, the future Maharishi turned to religion and spent the next 13 years as a disciple of Guru Dev. Supposedly he was charged with devising a simple meditation technique that would guarantee immediate results for the average person; by contrast, some of the regimens of yoga or Zen Buddhism demanded years of intense study and asceticism before benefits could be realized.

To complete his task he retired to a Himalayan cave for two years. At the end of this period, he assumed the title *Maharishi,* which in Sanskrit means "Great Seer." He called his system Transcendental Meditation.

TM created no great excitement in his native India, so the Maharishi moved his base of operations to the U.S., where he set up the Spiritual Regeneration Foundation in 1959. Later he formed the Students International Meditation Society (SIMS) to spread the TM gospel on college campuses. He assumed, perhaps rightly, that people in Western countries were more accustomed to accepting new ideas.

The Maharishi, a slight man with long hair and a beard, became a Hindu renunciant, or monk, as a follower of Guru Dev, and as such is both a celibate and a vegetarian. He now lives in Seelisberg, Switzerland, which he calls the "International Capital of the Age of Enlightenment."

In the early 1960s the Maharishi won some converts and newspaper headlines when actress Mia Farrow and the rock-music group the Beatles announced they had taken up TM. The Beatles spent several months in India studying with the master but eventually left the movement. Someone persuaded the Maharishi to tour the U.S. with a rock group called the Beach Boys: the tour flopped. He returned to India, and most people wrote TM off as one more fizzled fad.

A dedicated group of devotees continued to meditate and told themselves and their friends they felt much better, but they had no scientific evidence that TM really worked. The revival of interest in TM can be traced to the publication of scientific studies undertaken by a Ph.D. candidate in physiology at the University of California at Los Angeles in collaboration with Dr. Benson. R. Keith Wallace measured such things as blood pressure and heart-rate in a group of 27 meditators. Wallace and Benson reported that TM seemed to be a fourth state of consciousness, along with waking, dreaming, and sleeping. TM entered its second spring.

Some 6,000 certified TM teachers now staff more than 400 centers in the U.S. alone. The movement's goal is to train one teacher for each 1000 people. Each instructor receives at least part of his or her training from the Maharishi himself; ideally the TM teacher will spend six months in training and three months in field work.

Some early TM enthusiasts have become critical of the commercial aspects of the movement. In recent years the American branch alone has been taking in about $20 million annually in tax-exempt dollars — TM qualifies as a non-profit educational organization. A staff of 60 people directs the work of the three major TM organizations: the Students International Meditation Society, which is active on hundreds of campuses; the International Meditation Society; and the American Foundation for the Science of Creative Intelligence, which caters to businessmen.

The movement purchased the 185-acre campus of the bankrupt Parsons College in Fairfield, Iowa, in 1974 and renamed it Maharishi International University. The 800 enrolled students pay $3,000 a year for tuition (1980) and incorporate twice-daily meditation in a rigorous academic program. No liquor or recreational drugs are allowed, and the students go to bed by 10 p.m. College publications describe MIU as more than just another small college; they see it as a research institution dedicated to conquering stress in human society and bringing humankind to a state of "cosmic consciousness." Another TM university operates in Switzerland.

Advanced courses and retreats are given at the 460-acre, multimillion-dollar resort complex at Livingston Manor, N.Y. Large corporations (such as AT&T and General Foods) have sponsored TM programs for employees; the U.S. Army has used TM to combat alcoholism and drug addiction.

All fees go to the national headquarters, which returns half to local TM centers for salaries and expenses. The teachers themselves may live on as little as $300 a month, although for some this is not a full-time job.

Many entertainers and athletes have been TM boosters, including Joe Namath, Carol Burnett, Bill Walton, Peggy Lee, and Stevie Wonder. Major Gen. Franklin Davis, former commandant of the U.S. War College, serves on the MIU board of trustees. One of the best promotions for TM has been the series of appearances of the Maharishi on the *Merv Griffin* (TV) *Show*. Griffin has persuaded such fellow-meditators as Mary Tyler Moore and Clint Eastwood to appear on his programs. During the programs, the Maharishi sits cross-legged in his white robe, expounds his hopes for Transcendental Meditation, giggles, and fondles flowers. The next day TM centers across the country find lines of new customers waiting for the doors to open.

Rival gurus sometimes scoff at the Maharishi's simplified yoga. After one particular Merv Griffin show, Swami Vishnu Devananda sniffed: "Gathering celebrities to talk about meditation is like gathering barbers to discuss brain surgery."

My own introduction to TM came when I spotted an ad in a local newspaper announcing a free public lecture. Not many things are free these days, so I circled the day on the calendar. About 15 people came to the community center to hear a smiling young man explain the benefits of regular meditation. He emphasized that TM was a simple technique that anyone could learn in a few minutes; even doubters would find that it produced its results despite their skepticism. Echoing the Maharishi, he denied that TM was in any way a religion or that it called for any drastic change in lifestyle. He did mention that anyone desiring to go through the initiation was asked to abstain from "recreational" drugs for 15 days before the ceremony; tobacco and alcohol were not forbidden.

One matron asked if Transcendental Meditation had anything to do with sleeping on a bed of nails. The young man smiled and assured her that that more spectacular type of Indian spirituality was not what he was promoting. He admitted that some Americans were thrown off by the word "transcendental" and that others doubted that anything so worthwhile and healthful could come out of India.

The TM teacher waited for someone in the audience to ask what the program costs. An adult pays $125, but a married couple and all their children under 14 are charged a family rate of $200. College students get the same instruction for $65, and high-school students pay from $35 to $55. Children between ages four and ten are asked to contribute two-weeks allowance.

The speaker ended the one-hour presentation by extolling the multiple benefits of meditation: less anxiety and worry, lower blood pressure, clearer thinking, less dependence on tobacco and drugs, lower blood lactate, and better memory. He said there would be a second introductory lecture in two weeks and invited us to fill out postcards that he would mail to us as a reminder. But a frantic search through his attaché case failed to turn up the postcards, and he apologized for having left them on his desk at home. I wondered about the "better memory" claim, but was curious enough to plan to attend the second TM program.

Because of a scheduling conflict, I participated in the second program in a different setting, a room in the student union of a nearby state university. At least 45 people crowded the room, and all but a handful were college students. Two TM teachers reviewed the material of the first lecture and offered more details on enrollment procedures. A professor who wanted to know how many secret mantras there were and how the instructor matched mantra to student got the brush-off. Finally those still interested were invited to sign up for the coming initiation; at least half of those in the room signed up.

One of the more controversial aspects of TM is the mantra and the secrecy surrounding it. The mantra is a Sanskrit word, or rather a sound, which the meditator repeats silently during the morning and evening meditations. No meditator is supposed to repeat his or her mantra aloud, write it down, or reveal it to anyone, not even to a spouse. To do so is said to dilute its potency.

The Maharishi and TM officials refuse to reveal the number of mantras that the teachers parcel out, but there are apparently only 17. A few mantras have been revealed: *Sherim, Inga, Shiam, Ima, Ram Kirim,* and *Shri Ram.* One of the major responsibilities of the teacher is to choose a mantra "in tune with" the initiate's personality and nervous system; yet the amount of information on which the assignment is made is minimal: name, date of birth, occupation, general mental state, marital status, and number of children.

Many doctors who endorse the idea of a daily meditation-period scoff at the idea of a secret mantra and recommend the use of any pleasant-sounding word (such as "one" or "peace" or "love") as a perfectly adequate mantra. Medical investigators have shown that meditators who use such words derive as much benefit as do those with secret, TM-certified mantras. The object of the mental device is simply to break up logical thought-patterns during meditation.

Christians might favor the ancient "Jesus prayer" of the Eastern churches, as a version of TM. The person sits quietly with eyes closed and simply synchronizes his or her breathing pattern with the words "Jesus" and "Abba." This technique of prayerful meditation goes back to the earliest days of Christianity.

A new organization, the American Association of Physicians Practicing the Transcendental Meditation and TM-Sidhi Programs, claims to represent 5,000 M.D.s and is headed by a Stanford medical professor. These doctors say TM is useful in treating stress and psycho-somatic problems. Prof. Daniel Liebowitz says, "TM is not a religion, not a cult, not hypnosis — it's a health measure. It relieves stress." The association has asked the federal government to allocate more funds for TM research and to consider the cost of TM sessions as legitimate medical expenses for tax purposes.

TM teachers impart the mantra in a brief initiation ceremony conducted in Sanskrit. The initiate is told to bring six to twelve fresh flowers, two or three fresh fruits, and a clean white handkerchief. The initiate removes his or her shoes and enters a room that features a portrait of Guru Dev. The teacher lights candles and incense and places the gifts on the altar. The teacher then reveals the mantra, which the new meditator repeats aloud several times and then mentally for ten minutes or so.

At several later group-meetings, the initiates get further instruction in techniques and a chance to ask questions. If they wish, they may return for "checking" every month without further cost. They are also urged to attend weekend TM courses.

Mrs. Lyn Doyle of West Lafayette, Indiana, has been meditating since July

1975. She and her husband took instruction in TM together. "My most notice-able benefit has been increased energy," she reports. "Before taking up TM I used to be dead tired by the end of the working day. Now I meditate at 7:30 in the morning and as soon as I get home around 5:30. I find I have a lot more energy and much less tension." She is an editor, and her husband is a computer programmer. He says TM has improved his ability to think through problems.

All of their friends who have learned TM have stayed with it. "The fact that you have paid a substantial sum of money for TM instructions means that you are more likely to use the technique to get your money's worth," Mrs. Doyle comments. TM headquarters publishes no statistics on the number who continue to meditate a year or so after starting.

The authors of a three-part series on TM in *Psychology Today* (April 1974) concluded that TM helps some people to relax, does nothing for others, and is harmful to a few.

Most people seem to try TM for personal reasons. They want to ease tension or live life more fully or lower their blood pressure. Now that TM has become a booming business, the Maharishi sees it as a means of reforming the world. "If only one percent of the people in a city or nation practice Transcendental Medi-tation, the crime, sickness, and accident rates will go down," he predicts. Scien-tific evidence that TM can accomplish *those* results is not nearly so convicing as the evidence relating to its effect on practitioners' blood pressure.

Even TM devotees smile in embarrassment at some of the Maharishi's more extravagant claims, as well as at his painfully naïve political and economic views. The credibility of the TM movement has been strained by the Maharishi's announcement that meditators can now learn the techniques of levitation by paying hefty extra fees. The ordinary person can see that it is one thing to use TM to relax — but to fly around the room in defiance of the laws of gravity is something else.

Nevertheless levitators now claim that they can assume the crossed-legs lotus position and rise one or two feet and then move five to ten feet forward in a state of levitation. Practice rooms, closed to reporters and cameras, are equipped with foam-rubber mats. To date, the movement has refused to allow a public demon-stration of levitation; it has distributed some photographs, which outsiders view with skepticism.

Levitation costs far more than meditation. Meditators who want to learn to fly must enroll in a preparatory class of four to eight weeks at $245 a week, which includes room, board, and flying lessons. There follow four two-week courses at $375 a week. The total cost can thus approach $5,000, with no mon-ey-back guarantee if the trainee remains earthbound.

Dr. Herbert Spiegel, a psychiatrist who teaches at Columbia University, ex-plains the stories of levitation as examples of self-hypnosis. The "levitators" probably imagine that they have actually been flying; but, Dr. Spiegel says, "the law of gravity applies to everyone, regardless of creed, race, color, and TM."

TM lacks any particular ethical stance. It supposedly works for anyone, just as does an aspirin or tranquilizer. It would lessen the tension of a bank robber on the night before the heist, as well as that of a neighbor worrying about a pay raise. TM does not call for a change in lifestyles, or a conversion, or adherence to any moral code. As such its role in reforming society must be questioned. Efficiency alone is not the road to utopia, and TM simply tries to improve efficiency — of the Mafia don as well as of the medical missionary. Not that TM is therefore bad; it is simply morally neutral.

Do-it-yourself meditation probably works as well as TM, but the systematic program devised by the Maharishi has some elements conducive to success in a society such as that of the U.S. We often do place a higher value on something that costs a great deal of money. Furthermore, many people follow a program — whether it is Weight Watchers or tennis lessons or TM — only if they can count on group reinforcement and encouragement. Finally, although you can learn almost anything from a book — including ballroom dancing, chess, and swimming — you will probably learn more quickly with a personal instructor. And besides you can't ask a book questions.

A small library of books, some of them best-sellers, purport to explain TM; but readers soon discover that the authors refuse to delve into the business of the mantra, preferring to direct readers to the nearest TM center. Some authors even hint at the grave problems one may encounter if one tries to meditate without formal instruction. They relate horror stories about people who revealed their mantras or borrowed someone else's mantra. To which one might respond by asking: "If using the wrong mantra is so dangerous, what assurance do we have that TM teachers, in their early 20s with a few months' training, will infallibly prescribe the *right* mantra for *me?*"

If TM offers half the benefits many meditators report, it may well be worth the cost, which is still less than that of a day in a hospital. But those who are self-motivated can receive the same results by following the rules for meditation formulated by Dr. Benson. He claims that anyone can learn to meditate in five minutes. His technique includes four elements: a quiet environment, a mental device, a passive attitude, and a comfortable position. The procedure he recommends is this:

1. Pick a time before eating or at least two hours after eating; somehow the digestive process interferes with good meditation.

2. Select a quiet spot without distraction and sit comfortably in a chair; if you meditate lying down, you may simply fall asleep.

3. Close your eyes and relax your body starting from your toes and continuing to the top of your head.

4. *Adopt a simple mental device or word such as "one" and repeat this sound mentally every time you exhale.*

5. *Adopt a passive attitude. Do not concentrate on any subject or try to solve any problems but do not worry if your mind wanders. If you get too far afield, return to the mental repetition of your word.*

6. *Spend 15 to 20 minutes once or twice a day in meditation. After you finish meditating, open your eyes and sit quietly for a few minutes before going about your business.*

Dr. Benson has said that one 20-minute meditation can provide more deep rest than six hours of sleep; though meditation is not a substitute for sleep. Some people avoid meditating late in the evening because they get so much energy from it that they find themselves wide awake at 3 a.m.

Some of the medical investigations of the benefits of TM are impressive, but many have been too limited to be conclusive. Oxygen consumption does drop significantly during TM, but it also drops when a subject listens to 20 minutes of restful music. Evidence that TM improves creativity or memory is lacking. Much additional scientific investigation is needed.

Clearly TM or any other form of meditation to achieve relaxation or lower blood pressure is not the same as prayer or religious meditation. TM is no more a substitute for prayer than is a brisk walk or a tranquilizer. Christians may, however, be able to enrich their praying if they minimize deep-seated anxieties and tensions.

Christian observers differ on their evaluations of TM. The evangelical magazine *Christianity Today* charged (Sept. 12, 1975) that TM "is permeated with the Hindu life and worldview. Although it does not call for the robes and vegetarian diet of other Hindu imports, in the crucial concepts of God, man, sin, and fellowship between God and man, . . . TM is thoroughly Hinduistic."

A coalition of parents, Protestant fundamentalists, and civil libertarians filed suit in 1976 to stop the teaching of TM in New Jersey public schools. The head of Americans United for Separation of Church and State has called TM a "subtly disguised form of Hinduism." With the help of a $40,812 grant from the Department of Health, Education, and Welfare, the TM program has been offered in five New Jersey high schools, to see if its techniques can help students improve learning skills and modify behavior patterns. Upholding a lower court ruling, the U.S. Court of Appeals in Philadelphia declared in 1979 that Transcendental Meditation was religious in nature and, as such, should not be taught in public schools.

Many critics identify TM as a religion on the basis of a translation of the *puja*, the Sanskrit chant used during the initiation, and the Hindu meaning of the personalized mantras. They say the initiation involves "bowing down" to major Hindu deities.

Father Richard Mangini, editor of the *Catholic Voice* of Oakland, California, also takes a dim view of TM and insists that it is "absolutely crucial" for Catholics to recognize that its teachings "conflict with basic Christian teaching and Christian religious experience." On the other hand, Norris Clarke, S.J., professor of philosophy at Fordham University, has said that anyone can practice TM "regardless of religious belief" but should not expect TM to provide a complete philosophy and guide for life. "It's a technique to assist you in finding a meaning from elsewhere."

The Catholic may show more tolerance of the vestiges of Hinduism in TM than the fundamentalist Protestant. The Fathers of Vatican Council II chose not to condemn Hinduism but to show sympathy for Hindus who "seek release from the anguish of our condition through ascetical practices or deep meditation or a loving, trusting flight toward God."

Most Americans pay little attention to the Maharishi's own religious views, and have no idea what the short Sanskrit chant of the TM initiation may mean. Many Catholic priests, monks, nuns, and lay people, as well as Protestant ministers and laity, practice TM. For the great majority of Americans who practice TM, the goal is simply to find a simple technique to relieve stress. Yet for some the TM movement becomes a cult and a way of life grounded in the Hindu philosophy that inspires the Maharishi.

Whether through TM, or Dr. Benson's technique, or some other method, a person may discover that daily meditation can improve the quality of emotional, as well as physical, life. It evidently can provide the sort of tonic for the mind that physical exercise does for the body.

CHAPTER X

The Hare Krishna Movement

Transplanted Hindu sect promises
salvation through chanting.

Some of the cults examined in this book were born in the 20th century. But the Hare Krishna movement originated in the 15th century. It was introduced into the U.S. only in 1965.

Essentially considered, the International Society for Krishna Consciousness (ISKCON) is the Western version of a fundamentalist Hindu sect. Its devotees attract attention by their shaved heads and peculiar garb and their chanting of the Hare Krishna mantra on city streets. They are popularly known as Hare Krishnas *(hah-ray krish-nahz)*.

The American members of ISKCON, usually products of middle-class homes and sometimes refugees from the drug culture, adopt a way of life as far removed from the customs and values of the larger society as that of any contemporary cult. Monks shave their heads save for a top-knot, and wear saffron robes and sandles; women devotees wear the traditional Indian sari. All wear white-clay marks on their foreheads, which designate a follower of Krishna. They give up meat, fish, eggs, illicit sex, alcohol, coffee, tea, gambling, and drugs. Their daily routine, from arising at 3:34 a.m. to lights out at 10 p.m., is devoted to praising Krishna, the Supreme Personality of the Godhead — and seeking converts and funds.

The several thousand committed members in the U.S. live in about 30 temples, located in New York, San Francisco, Los Angeles, and other major cities. Others follow the Hare Krishna path in India and a score of foreign cities. Besides the dozen or so cultists who live in each temple, several times that number hold secular jobs, attend meetings and eat meals at the temple, and provide financial support. The American society alone is said to have an annual income of more than $20 million.

Often wearing toupees and street clothes, about 100 Hare Krishnas haunt the nation's air terminals and solicit travelers. They try to sell copies of their books or their *Back to Godhead* magazine (500,000 copies per issue) to people generally far more interested in getting their persons and baggage on a scheduled flight. Targeting such prospects as young men, the military, and businessmen, a devotee can bring in, on average, $100 a day in sales and contributions. Others "work" suburban shopping centers, downtown streets, and campuses. During the Christmas season Hare Krishna cultists have taken to wearing Santa Claus suits on city streets; most shoppers who contribute probably think they are giving to the Salvation Army.

Despite the commercial impression it conveys to many, ISKCON has genuine spiritual roots. Devotees worship Krishna as the Supreme Lord of the Hindu pantheon of deities. In this respect they differ from the impersonalist Vedantists, the other Western interpretation of Hinduism that has won some American converts.

Their specific religious beliefs go back to Chaitanya Mahaprabhu (b. 1486), whom they believe to be one of the many incarnations of Krishna. In his first incarnation, Krishna, it is said, appeared in India about 5,000 years ago and taught his disciple Arjuna. Chaitanya taught that men reach spiritual bliss not by good works or meditation but by chanting the name of Krishna to the point of spiritual ecstacy. The founder of the Krishnaite sect won followers in Bengal and northeast India; and his movement became established as one of the numberless Hindu sects.

A writer in their magazine, *Back to Godhead,* explains the potency of the mantra: "The words Hare, Krishna, and Rama have a special quality because they are seeds of pure spiritual consciousness. They are not a product of an earthbound language changing through the centuries. They are the names of God, as ceaselessly energetic as God Himself. When you pronounce these sounds, you are propelled into your eternal position as a particle of spiritual energy, a person living in a transcendental nature. Hare Krishna reveals to you the person you really are" (vol. II.2, p. 1).

The typical Hindu beliefs in *karma* and in reincarnation remained basic doctrines of the Krishnaite sect. "As the embodied soul continually passes, in this body, from boyhood to youth to old age, the soul similarly passes into another body at death," explained the guru who brought the sect to American shores.

In an interview with a South African Reporter, Swami Bhaktivedanta elaborated his views on reincarnation. He said that each individual gets another body at the moment of death, but that the body may not be a human one. The swami said there are 8,400,000 different forms of life, and an individual can enter any one of them according to his or her mental condition at death. "If we cultivate the mode of goodness, then we are promoted to the higher planetary system, where there is a better standard of life. If we cultivate the mode of passion, then we will remain at the present stage. But if out of ignorance we commit sinful activities and violate nature's laws, then we will be degraded to animal or plant life. Then again we must evolve to the human form, a process that may take millions of years" (*Back to Godhead*, II.2, p. 5).

Traditional Hinduism outlines three ways to escape the endless cycle of reincarnations: by doing good works and performing acts of charity (Karma yoga), by gaining knowledge through meditation (Juana yoga), or by devotion to God (Bhakti yoga). ISKCON advocates the third (or Bhakti yoga) course.

His Divine Grace A. C. Bhaktivedanta Swami Prabupada was born in Calcutta in 1896. He studied at the University of Calcutta and was employed by an Indian chemical company until his retirement. With meager resources he started the English-language *Back to Godhead* magazine in 1944. In 1950, at the age of 54, he left his wife and five children and became a monk to seek spiritual enlightenment. His own guru instructed him to bring Krishna Consciousness to the Western world, and he set off by freighter for New York City. There he sat under a tree in Tompkins Park on the Lower East Side until his chanting of the Hare Krishna mantra began to attract a small band of hippies. They formed the nucleus of the International Society for Krishna Consciousness, founded in 1966.

From New York the cult spread to the Haight-Ashbury section of San Francisco and then to other American cities. The swami ignored the advice of other Hindu teachers in the U.S. to Westernize his teachings by allowing the wearing of suits and ties and the eating of meat; he was determined to present unadultered Krishnaism. The cult got added publicity from its street performances, the composition "My Sweet Lord" by George Harrison of the Beatles, and the appearance of Hare Krishna chanters in the stage-musical *Hair* (1967). Hundreds of young Americans, mostly in their 20s, exchanged the "high" they had been getting from drugs for the spiritual "high" that came from incessant chanting and dancing. The poet Allen Ginsberg was among those who joined in the chanting.

Eventually the cult bought a former Methodist church in Los Angeles; it became home for 60 members, as well as national headquarters. In the 1970s, ISKCON dedicated a $2 million temple in Bombay; the temple includes a hotel, library, and theater.

Some 200 members (including 60 children) operate New Vrindaban, a 2,000-acre farm in the hills of West Virginia. Almost 15,000 people attended the dedication of the "Palace of Gold" temple there on Labor Day weekend in 1980. Construction was done by 60 Hare Krishna workmen who taught themselves the necessary building skills. Some $500,000 was spent on imported marble, teakwood, onyx, gold and copper leaf, stained glass, and 42 crystal chandeliers. One of the two main devotional rooms features a life-like wax figure of the swami. Plans call for the addition of a vegetarian restaurant, museum, formal gardens, and six more temples. But Vrindaban is not easily accessible to tourists; it is situated four miles from the nearest highway, with the only access by one narrow dirt road.

The cult receives funds from several sources: the assets of new members, profits from the sale of incense, books, and magazines, and donations from fellow travelers and the general public. Their Spiritual Sky Scented Products Company in Los Angeles, the largest U.S. incense manufacturer, earns a profit of more than $1 million a year (1980). It also distributes organic suntan lotion, shampoo, and body oils.

Life for the "inner circle" — those who live in the temples — is highly structured. New members spend six months in the novitiate and then receive Hindu names and the first of many initiations. From rising to bedtime, they follow a set schedule, which includes chanting, meditation, reading, eating, temple cleaning, work, two showers, and worship. Each temple is decorated with statues of various Hindu deities, paintings of Krishna, and a large portrait of His Divine Grace.

Prominent in the liturgy of the cult is the *artika* ceremony, which is open to visitors as well as cultists. Devotees offer a candle to the Hindu deities represented by statues. They go through an orgy of singing, dancing, and chanting that seems to end in an altered state of consciousness. In another rite, the Hare Krishnas touch the floor with their foreheads in worship of the Tulasi bush; they present flowers and incense to the bush.

Strict segregation of the sexes is prescribed for the unmarried. Women cultists are told to look at a man's feet instead of his eyes, and to walk two steps behind the men. They are also forbidden to be alone with a man. Although lifelong celibacy is encouraged, most Krishnas eventually marry and have children. Married couples may engage in sexual intercourse only once a month — at the time when conception is most likely. In this they follow the precept of Swami Bhaktivedanta, who decreed, "Sex life, according to religious principles (*dharma*), should be for the propagation of children, not otherwise" (*Bhagavad-Gita As It Is*, p. 127).

Women are expected to be completely subservient to male devotees. The swami explained: "As children are very prone to be misled, women are also very prone to degradation. Therefore, both children and women require protection by the elder members of the family. By being engaged in various religious practices, women will not be misled into adultery. According to the sage Canakya Pandita, women are generally not very intelligent and therefore not trustworthy" (p. 14).

The cult recruits most of its converts from among the young people who accept an invitation to attend a lecture or Sunday meal at the temple. The exotic vegetarian meals, clouds of incense, strange chanting, garish paintings and statues, and earnest preaching lure a certain number to continue their investigation and possibly cast their lot with Lord Krishna. Some may choose to live in the commune, while others may retain their secular occupations but contribute funds to the Hare Krishna activities.

Within 20 years the Hare Krishna movement had established centers in Ann Arbor, Atlanta, Baltimore, Berkeley, Boston, Buffalo, Charlotte, Chicago, Cleveland, Dallas, Denver, Detroit, Gainesville, Honolulu, Houston, Las Vegas, Los Angeles, Miami, New Orleans, New York, Philadelphia, Phoenix, Pittsburgh, Portland, St. Louis, San Diego, San Francisco, Seattle, and Washington, D.C.

Centers have also been formed in such overseas cities as Amsterdam, Berlin, Geneva, London, Paris, Rome, Buenos Aires, Mexico City, and Melbourne, as well as a number in India.

The votaries employ all their senses in praising Krishna. They wear a sort of rosary of 108 prayer-beads and are expected to complete 16 rounds a day reciting the name of Krishna. They hear the reading and exposition of the Hindu scriptures and memorize prayers in Bengali and Sanskrit. They partake of the *prasadam,* or love feasts; all meals are vegetarian and must be prepared according to Hindu "kosher" regulations. They view the statues of the various deities in the temple, which are daily bathed and dressed. They smell the incense pervading the temple.

The *Back to Godhead* magazine gives this rationale for the cult's insistence on vegetarianism: "The strict law of karma deals measure for measure with anyone who violates the laws of nature. As long as the people of the world continue to murder and eat their most benign friends, the cow and the bull, they will perpetually suffer the sinful reactions of criminal violence and catastrophic wars" (II.1). The cult teaches that the vast majority of people are involved in *maya,* the pursuit of material pleasures. But the few who cultivate Krishna Consciousness enjoy transcendental pleasure far surpassing any material pleasures of the world.

The basic philosophy of the ISKCON is summarized in these eight principles:

1. *By sincerely cultivating a bona fide spiritual science, we can be free from anxiety and come to a state of pure, unending, blissful consciousness.*

2. *We are not our bodies but eternal spirit souls, parts and parcels of God (Krishna). As such, we are all brothers, and Krishna is ultimately our common father.*

3. *Kirshna is the eternal, all-knowing, omnipresent, all-powerful, and all-attractive Personality of Godhead. He is the seed-giving father of all living beings, and He is the sustaining energy of the entire cosmic creation.*

4. *The Absolute Truth is contained in all the great scriptures of the world. However, the oldest known revealed scriptures in existence are the Vedic literatures, most notably the* Bhagavad-gītā, *which is the literal record of God's actual words.*

5. *We should learn the Vedic knowledge from a genuine spiritual master — one who has no selfish motives and whose mind is firmly fixed on Lord Krishna.*

6. *Before we eat, we should offer to the Lord the food that sustains us. Then Krishna becomes the offering and purifies us.*

7. *We should perform all our actions as offerings to Krishna and do nothing for our own sense gratification.*

8. *The recommended means for achieving the mature stage of love of God in this age of Kali, or quarrel, is to chant the holy names of the Lord. The easiest method for most people is to chant the Hare Krishna mantra: Hare Krishna, Hare Krishna, Krishna Krishna Krishna, Hare Hare/Hare Rāma, Hare Rāma, Rāma Rāma, Hare Hare.*

Members of the cult believe that Krishna is also the god of Judaism, Christianity, and Islam under another name, a personal god. They even find a place for Jesus and the Christian Bible, but not in a sense that would satisfy orthodox Christians.

Bhaktivedanta's translation and commentary on *Bhagavad-Gita* serves as the cult's bible. While sophisticated Hindus view the Vedas and *Bhagavad-Gita* as largely allegorical and mythical, the Hare Krishnas accept them as literally true. It would not occur to a devotee to apply the principles of higher textual criticism to these sacred texts.

Swami Bhaktivedanta had harsh words for another Eastern savant, the Maharishi, and his Transcendental Meditation. "Their meditation is simply a farce — another cheating process by the so-called *swamis* and *yogis.* . . . These bluffers use the word 'meditation' but they do not know the proper subject for meditation. They're simply talking bogus propaganda. . . . Unfortunately, in the name of God consciousness or 'self-realization' many bluffers are presenting nonstandard methods of meditation without referring to the authorized books of Vedic knowledge. They are simply practicing another type of exploitation."

Some American young people have no doubt been attracted to the Hare

Krishna cult after disillusionment with the promiscuity, materialism, nihilism, and drug addiction of their former lives. Some may have been drawn to its non-violence and anti-intellectualism. Like many other contemporary cults, ISKCON offers the sort of supportive community that many converts found lacking in their homes, churches, and schools. Once drawn into its life, the devotees find themselves on a treadmill of activities that leave no room for reflection.

Like many contemporary cults, ISKCON leads the votary to focus inwardly. It displays no interest in works of charity, much less in social reform.

The full impact of Bhaktivedanta's death in 1977 remains to be seen. Of the many young people now dancing and chanting on the streets, some will no doubt live their lives as Hare Krishna devotees, and others will come to look upon the time they spent in the temple as simply a strange interlude in their lives. The cult's asceticism, alienation from the larger society, and brainwashing techniques have led some cultists to reconsider their commitment. Some have returned to their families only after forced deprogramming. In any event, the movement brought to these shores by Bhaktivedanta Swami Prabhupada has become one of the more exotic religious cults, as well as one of the few Hindu sects to win any sizeable Western following.

CHAPTER XI

The Children of God

Moses David: modern prophet or dirty old man?

Springing from the unlikely soil of the U.S. counterculture in the late 1960s were dozens of small Protestant groups whose adherents were popularly known as Jesus People (or Jesus Freaks). Many converts had left a life of drug addiction and sexual promiscuity to embrace an ascetic and enthusiastic brand of Christianity. Their new lives revolved around intense Bible study and the search for new recruits. One of these groups called itself The Children of God (COG).

The movement started in a teen-age coffee house in Huntington Beach, California. A one-time Christian and Missionary Alliance minister and free-lance evangelist, David Berg, opened the center in 1968 and called his ministry "Teens for Christ." His programs attracted dozens of hippies and other young people who had abandoned drugs in favor of the old-time religion.

Originally Berg encouraged his Teens for Christ to memorize large chunks of the Bible, pray, work, and witness. A neophyte was expected to learn 300 Bible verses by heart during the first two months and to add two more verses every day thereafter. Up at 6:45 a.m. and to bed by 11:30 p.m., the initiates followed a highly structured regimen. Forbidden were sex outside of marriage and use of drugs. Yet they bore little resemblance to conventional Christians. The *National Observer* published a report that the Children of God "roamed streets and beaches in sackcloth, faces daubed with ashes, yokes hanging from their necks, exhorting the unsaved to come to Jesus before it was too late." Members of the COG also engaged in speaking in tongues and healing, evidence of its Pentecostal orientation.

They viewed themselves as the only 100-percent Christians, those who had forsaken all to follow Jesus. They scorned secular knowledge and limited their reading to the Bible. According to Berg, the King James Version was the only inspired version (a pronouncement that has presented a problem to those whose native language is not English).

But in a short time, other less-Christian influences began to change the Children of God. Warned by his mother, who was a radio evangelist and reputed prophetess, and impelled by his own faith in astrology, Berg became convinced that California was about to fall into the ocean. He shuttered the coffee shop and packed his band of 50 or 60 followers into vans, which headed east to warn the rest of the country of the impending disaster.

When the caravan reached northern Illinois, Berg divided the members into 12 tribes and gave each person an Old Testament name. Berg, who claims to be of Jewish ancestry, became Moses David. A newspaper reporter applied the label "Children of God" to the cult, and Berg appropiated the name for his movement. (It sometimes goes also by the name Family of Love.)

Moses David Berg decided to join forces with Fred Jordan, a radio and TV preacher with whom he had once been associated. The Children of God headed for three properties owned by Jordan and his Soul Clinic ministry: a 400-acre ranch some 70 miles from Fort Worth, Texas; a rescue mission on Los Angeles' skid row; and a ranch near Coachella, California. Both of the evangelists gained from their alliance. Berg had a chance to consolidate his power in the cult, and Jordan could boast that his evangelistic efforts were winning hundreds of young people for Jesus.

But Berg and his Children were too radical and left-wing for the conservative Jordan, who evicted the entire group in the fall of 1971. By this time the COG numbered about 1,000 members. They scattered to set up communes in New York, Seattle, Dallas, Detroit, and other cities. Several bands of other Jesus Freaks joined forces with the Children of God, and the cult began to receive national TV and newspaper coverage.

One sure-fire publicity technique that brought attention to the cult was to invade a mainline Protestant church on Sunday morning and disrupt worship by shouting obscenities and calling parishioners to repentance. The nation's Methodists and Baptists began to see that the Children of God were more than just exuberant converts from the counterculture.

Although married, Berg was living with his secretary, Maria. Later he would take additional concubines, citing as precedent the marital pattern of Abraham, Solomon, and David. On the basis of Acts 2.44 (which explains that the early Christians held all things in common), he promoted wife-swapping among the COG. Moses David joined the sexual revolution and eventually advocated polygamy, incest, premarital sex, religious prostitution, and sexual activity for schoolchildren. His kinky ideas finally found their way into the press.

Moses David communicates with his disciples around the world by means of "MO letters." In an early letter he explained that the Old Church was based on the inspired word for yesterday — the Bible — whereas the New Church would be built on God's word for today — the MO letters. He had issued more than 500 letters by the end of 1980, increasingly pornographic in content. He prepares at least three versions of these letters: one to the inner core, another to the ordinary followers, and a third to the newcomers and the general public.

The Bible still plays a role in the COG, but it is obviously a secondary one. In a 1973 MO letter, titled *Old Battles,* Berg wrote: "I want to frankly tell you, if there is a choice between reading your Bible, I want to tell you that you better read what God said today, in preference to what he said 2,000 to 4,000 years ago. Then when you've gotten done reading the latest MO letters, you can go back to reading the Bible."

The sale of these MO letters forms an important source of income for Berg and the cult. Printed for pennies and sold for donations of a nickel to a dollar, more than 4 million MO letters are distributed each month. An active American colony of the COG can bring in between $2,500 and $5,000 a week from begging and sale of the letters. Outsiders are told they are giving financial support to a drug-rehabilitation program or a youth center.

The Christian churches were not the only object of Berg's increasing hatred. He grew more and more anti-American and often referred to the United States as "America the Whore." In the mid-1970s he predicted that the Comet Kohoutek was headed straight for the American continent. To escape the catastrophe, Berg closed most of the 100 U.S. colonies (communes) and told his followers to resettle in Europe, Latin America, Australia, and other countries. Only a couple of thousand Children remain in the U.S.

A study by the Anti-Defamation League of B'nai B'rith charged that the cult is also anti-Semitic. Berg regularly refers to Jews as "Christ killers" and maintains that Jews control the news media and have formed an international conspiracy of bankers.

One famous MO letter (March 1974) pictures a mermaid making love to a naked man, with the caption "Hooker for Jesus." The letter, entitled *Flirty Little Fishy,* urged the female Children to seduce potential converts. This religious prostitution has led to an epidemic of venereal disease and illegitimate births in the colonies.

In a letter entitled *God's Love Slave* (1974), Moses relates how he gave his concubine Maria to a number of men and then questioned her afterward to learn details of her love-making experience.

Berg approves of lesbianism but not male homosexuality. In *Women in Love,* a 1973 letter, he wrote: "Male homosexuality is expressly, definitely and specifically *forbidden* and *cursed* and called *sodomy.* In that case it is absolutely forbidden and a *sin.* But I don't see and I've never been able to find any place in the Bible where it is forbidden to *women.*"

In its early days, the cult baptized converts by immersion; but baptisms are now rare. Occasionally a cultist will get some wine and bread and hold a communion service.

Berg's eschatology resembles that of Jehovah's Witnesses and similar adventist sects. The Antichrist will soon appear and almost overwhelm the forces of God, but Christ will return and reign for 1,000 years. Satan will launch one more rebellion but will ultimately be vanquished. In the end everyone will be saved, including Satan. The MO letters predict the end of the world as we know it in about 1993.

From the beginning the Children of God were expected to "forsake all" and follow their new faith. Consequently they had to cut all ties with family and friends. Their possessions were to be turned over to the cult, as would any income they might receive.

Children of God once lived in communes with as many as 150 members; but now colonies are limited to a maximum of a dozen. The colony becomes their only home, and exists in several varieties: the Basic Front Line Colonies, Publishing Colonies, Widows Colonies, and so forth. Berg has even authorized Catacombs Colonies for youngsters who cannot yet leave home to join a regular colony; they meet weekly to study MO letters. Despite the free-sex activities of the cult, members are forbidden to use drugs or tobacco.

Distraught parents of COG members have formed FREECOG (Free Our Children from the Children of God). The leader of these parents is a former U.S. Navy officer from San Diego whose own daughter, a nurse, had become involved with the cult. Scores of parents have also hired Ted Patrick, a professional deprogrammer, to kidnap their sons and daughters from COG colonies.

Berg, now 60, lives in seclusion in Europe; most members of the cult have never seen him. Reputedly he has also lived in the Canary Islands and in Libya. Ex-members say he is frail, sometimes sports a goatee, and impresses visitors with piercing eyes. One of his sons, Paul, died under strange circumstances in the Swiss Alps in 1973; he either fell or jumped from a cliff.

Berg stands at the top of the cult's authority-pyramid. Under him are several prime ministers and a number of ministers, archbishops, bishops, regional shepherds, and district shepherds. At the bottom are the ordinary disciples and babes (novices).

In directing the worldwide affairs of the cult, Berg says he is able to call on "spiritual counselors" who are spirits willing to share their wisdom. Chief among these is one Abrahim, who is supposed to be a gypsy king who died a thousand years ago. Other regular counselors who visit Moses David include Rasputin, Joan of Arc, Oliver Cromwell, Martin Luther, and William Jennings Bryan. Moses David also reports having had sexual encounters with lady spirits called "goddesses."

New York State's Attorney General Louis J. Lefkowitz conducted an 18-month investigation of the Children of God and issued a 65-page report in 1974. He and his committee took testimony from current and former members, parents, and scholars. The report accused the cult of fraud, tax evasion, brainwashing, imprisoning, and sexually abusing young converts. Referring to Berg, Herbert J. Wallenstein, head of the New York investigation, stated: "His letters are blatantly pornographic, complete with sketches and diagrams."

In 1977 the Children of God were startled to receive a mysterious letter entitled "God Bless You — And: Good-bye," in which Berg supposedly confesses that he has been a false prophet. A later tape recording from Berg called the letter "a completely fraudulant and lying forgery, rather shabbily concocted by some crackpot who is apparently partially demented." In the same tape recording, Berg said the circulation of the fake letter only showed "what slimy stinking depths our enemies do not hesitate to slither to try to stop us, including criminal acts of kidnapping, involuntary incarceration, mental and physical torture and even murder!"

Berg conducted a purge of top officials in 1978; among those who left or were banished were his daughter Linda, her ex-husband Jethro, and his legal wife, Jane. *Christianity Today* reported that total membership in the COG fell from 8,068 in January 1978 to 4,958 in May 1979. Berg has also changed the name of the cult from Children of God to Family of Love; but the group is still generally known by its original name.

Since leaving the U.S., the Children of God have become what *Time* magazine has called "a brigade of international nomads." Recently Berg issued a MO letter to his nomad followers in which he signaled a new strategy to advance his longstanding anti-Catholicism: "We are now beginning to invade the Catholic countries of the world and we are going to have to be pro-Catholic. . . . They believe much the same as we do! They also believe in communes, in forsaking all, in brainwashing and memorization! . . . Go partake of their little Eucharist, go kneel with them in their chapels. . . . They don't know anything else. . . . Play along with them. . . . Join the circus."

Berg believes "the system" is engaged in persecuting his followers. In a MO letter dated Dec. 31, 1978, he wrote: "Beloved, we have had our good years! — our fat years and our famous years! . . . I believe that we're now entering into our worldwide persecution lean years. Jonestown is their excuse to attack all the cults, and the cults are their excuse to attack us! Because there is not one of them that preaches Christ like we do."

Moses David seems now to pattern his life more on that of *Playboy* magazine publisher Hugh Hefner than on that of Jesus Christ. The hundreds of MO letters have supplanted the Bible as the cult's authoritative scriptures; and Berg's strange mixture of astrology, spiritualism, palm reading, Christianity, and sexual license has become the cult's new gospel.

Chapter XII

The Way

Victor Paul Wierwille tells followers that
he rediscovered 1st-century Christianity.

If one had to summarize the theological outlook of Victor Paul Wierwille in a couple of words, one might justifiably call him a Pentecostal unitarian. This ex-minister of the Evangelical and Reformed Church (now the United Church of Christ) maintains that God has spoken to him audibly and revealed the true understanding of the Bible and Christianity, lost since the early days of the Church.

The movement that has grown from Wierwille's heterodox doctrines has attracted an estimated 40,000 members, mostly young people, in the 50 states and as many foreign countries. His ideas are energetically propagated by a corps of missionaries, a college in Kansas, a Bible school in Indiana, a course of instruction on cassette recordings, a magazine, and a small library of books that he has authored. The cult is known as The Way.

Wierwille, born in 1916, was raised in a fundamentalist home. A few years after leaving high school, he married his childhood sweetheart, who had just finished nursing training. He attended Mission House College and Seminary in Sheboygan, Wisconsin, and later received a master's degree in practical theology from Princeton. Some correspondence courses in the Bible, from the Moody Bible Institute of Chicago, completed his formal theological education. Wierwille regularly uses the title "Dr." (he received an academic doctorate from an unaccredited, now defunct institution called Pike's Peak Theological Seminary, which was generally known as a "diploma mill").

Ordained in 1941, the new minister accepted the pastorate of a small Evangelical and Reformed church in Payne, Ohio, which he served for three years. He then took over a congregation of 21 active members in nearby Van Wert. It was while he was serving the Van Wert church that Wierwille began to question several basic tenets of his Protestant faith. At one point he toted several hundred volumes from his personal library to the local dump; he vowed to ground his belief-system solely on the Bible as the literal and inerrant word of God.

The young clergyman also grew discouraged about the effectiveness of his work. He would later write: "As I looked about me at the communities where I had worked, the abundant life was frequently not evident. In contrast to these Christian people, I could see that the secular world of non-Christians was manifesting a more abundant life than were the members of the church." Wierwille put together a course he entitled "Power for Abundant Living" (PFAL), and in 1957 he quit the ministry of his denomination and started to devote his time to spreading his new understanding of Christianity. He moved to the 147-acre family farm in New Knoxville, Ohio, which is now headquarters for The Way International.

The founder of The Way maintains that God spoke audibly to him: "God told me if I would teach the Word, He would teach it to me as it hasn't been taught since the first century." He tells devotees of The Way that he alone presents the "pure and correct" interpretation of the Scriptures.

One of the cornerstones of Wierwille's theology (and the title of his most popular book) is: "Jesus Christ is not God." He attributes the adoption of the doctrine of the Trinity to a minority of bishops at the Council of Nicea in 325 A.D. and considers this doctrine the major error of Protestant and Catholic theology. The Way teaches that Jesus Christ is neither co-equal nor co-eternal with God, but is a created being. In this belief The Way aligns itself with the ancient Arians, as well as with other antitrinitarian sects, such as Jehovah's Witnesses and members of the Worldwide Church of God.

To win a hearing from possible converts, The Way often presents itself as simply a Bible-study group. Some young people may become deeply involved in the cult's activities before they recognize the gulf that separates The Way from orthodox Protestant and Catholic doctrines. Even then, as Wierwille says, "many people may be misled because while using the same language or words, we don't mean the same thing" (*Jesus Christ Is Not God*, p. 4).

According to Wierwille, Jesus was born of the Virgin Mary through the miraculous intervention of God but did not exist before his birth except in the mind of God. Mary remained a virgin until the conception of Jesus, but not until his birth. Jesus was only a perfect man, and the Holy Spirit is simply another name for God. According to The Way's founder these concepts are plainly taught in the Bible and formed the faith of the early Christians before a group of bishops at the Council of Nicea foisted the doctrine of the Trinity on the Church.

The Way teaches that Adam had a body, a soul, and a spirit. Through the sin of Adam and Eve, humans lost the spirit and, like animals and plants, were left with only a body and a soul. Wierwille explains that the body is the physical body, the soul is the life principle that humans share with other living creatures, and the spirit is "God's image." At the time of creation, God legally deeded the world to Adam; but after the Fall, Adam transferred the deed to Satan. To rectify this situation, God needed the assistance of a man — and it was this perfect man, Jesus Christ, who legally won the world back from Satan.

Through his life and death, Jesus opened the way for man to receive "holy spirit" (no article and no capital letters). People can get holy spirit through a proper understanding of the Bible, which they achieve with Wierwille's guidance. And, says Wierwille, "the manifestation of the spirit which produces true worship is speaking in tongues."

Specific instructions in speaking in tongues are given in the 15 three-hour taped sessions that form the "Power for Abundant Living" course. Initiates pay about $200 in advance for the PFAL program offered in the 1,500 Twigs (or local fellowships). They may not take notes during the sessions nor ask any questions until the end of the course.

Devotees of The Way practice glossolalia daily, sometimes for hours. Speaking in tongues is featured at all meetings of the cult, as are the other charismatic gifts of interpretation, healing, prophecy, and so on.

Members are constantly urged to "divide" or interpret the Bible. The movement considers the King James Version the only correct one. Wierwille believes that the Old Testament and the Gospels are intended for the Jews and gentiles, but that the rest of the New Testament is for born-again believers. The Way accordingly concentrates on the nine letters of St. Paul. This position, held by other small sects as well, is technically known as dispensationalism. It traces the start of the Church to the writing of the Pauline epistles.

An estimated 1,000 young people and a few adults sign up for the PFAL courses each month. Additional courses, at extra cost, are offered to those who successfully complete the introductory program.

Wierwille's organization registered only moderate growth until he attracted several leaders of the Jesus Movement in the late 1960s. The target of The Way has been the college campus; the missionary outreach has been mainly to white, middle-class young people between ages 18 and 24. Some older people do complete the PFAL course and affiliate with the movement, but estimates put 80 percent of the current membership (1980) under age 25.

The founder introduced a "tree-structure" for the cult in 1971, and his organizational abilities have fostered the remarkable growth of The Way. Headquarters, at New Knoxville, is known as the Roots; a region in the country is the Trunk; a state unit is a Limb; and a city organization, a Branch. Two or more members comprise a Twig, while individual members are called Leaves. Wierwille stands at the top of the pyramid of authority; he serves as president of the three-person board of directors.

Promotional literature distributed by The Way describes the movement as a "biblical research and teaching organization concerned with setting before men and women . . . the inherent accuracy of the Word of God. The Way is not a church, nor is it a denomination or a religious sect of any sort." Few impartial observers would take this disavowal at face value, for The Way has already ordained 50 men and women as Way ministers who perform all the functions of any minister, including conducting worship and performing marriages. Converts to the cult learn that there is a basic incompatibility between what they hear in The Way and what they have heard before in their own Methodist or Baptist churches. Once committed to the network of The Way, they soon give up their former church loyalties.

The life of a dedicated follower of The Way revolves around daily meetings, the breaking of the bread (Lord's Supper), and witnessing. All members are expected to tithe their incomes, and all tithe monies go to the New Knoxville headquarters.

In 1975 The Way purchased the property of a former United Presbyterian college in Emporia, Kansas, which now serves as the chief training center for the cult's missionaries and ministers. Wierwille spent $3 million for the property and remodeling. His son, Donald, a former elementary-school principal, was installed as the president of the college.

About 500 students attend the Emporia school, now known as The Way College, and most of these are preparing to become members of the Way Corps. They spend two years on the campus and two years on mission assignments seeking enrollments for the PFAL course and converts. Their parents or other sponsors pay the room, board, and tuition costs; students are not allowed to work while in school. In the field they are expected to find part-time jobs to support themselves, and to tithe their income.

Another group of dedicated Way members are known as Word Over the World (WOWS). They too support themselves while seeking converts to the cult. They agree to serve in this assignment for one year, and many then enroll in The Way College. Some 300 men and women staff the printing plant at New Knoxville, handle the correspondence courses, and prepare the audio-visual materials. They serve without pay.

The Way also operates a College of Biblical Research at Rome City, Indiana, and a Total Fitness Institute in the California Sierras. At the Institute, members undergo a two-week program that combines survival skills and Scripture study.

Wierwille usually preaches at a Sunday evening service at the Roots, but The Way prescribes no special day for worship. The cult considers Pentecost the chief holy day of the Christian year, relegating Easter and Christmas to secondary status.

The Way does not practice water baptism, because, as Wierwille explains: "to say that there is water involved in baptism can only be private interpretation" (*The Bible Tells Me So*, p. 135). Wierwille denies the authenticity of the Trinitarian formula for baptism in Matthew 28.19.

Like Jehovah's Witnesses, The Way teaches that Jesus died on a "torture stake" rather than on a cross. Furthermore, Wierwille maintains that Jesus died and was buried on a Wednesday and rose on Saturday; that he did not die between two thieves but between four other condemned men: the two robbers mentioned in Matthew and the two criminals in Luke. Like the Witnesses and the Worldwide Church of God, The Way teaches that man is not immortal; the dead remain dead until the final resurrection.

The main products of the New Knoxville printing plant are Wierwille's nine books, published under the American Christian Press imprint. *The Way* magazine reports more than 10,000 subscribers. Wierwille's teachings are also disseminated by other periodicals, such as *Heart: Testimonies of God's Deliverance*, and by TV programs and exhibits.

Each summer, on the county fairgrounds, The Way sponsors a Rock of Ages festival near New Knoxville, which serves as a national convention. At the 1980 festival, some 15,000 people paid $25 apiece for admission to hear gospel-rock bands, the 500-voice Way Chorale International, and preaching. Sometimes Wierwille tools around the fairgrounds on his Harley-Davidson motorcyle or in his golf cart.

Casual observers of the campus religious scene sometimes confuse The Way with such groups as Campus Crusade for Christ, Inter-Varsity Christian Fellowship, or The Navigators. But the theological inventions of Victor Paul Wierwille contrast sharply with the beliefs of those evangelical Protestant organizations. The Way displays more of the distinguishing marks of a contemporary cult than it does of 1st-century Christianity.

CHAPTER XIII

The Divine Light Mission

Guru Maharaj Ji announced his Divinity at age eight.

For 40 years, Paran Sant Satgurudev Shri Hans Ji Maharaj had labored in India to win followers to his version of Hinduism, which went under the name of Divine Light Mission. His missionary activities began in north India and West Pakistan in the early 1920s. By the time he died, in 1966, he was revered as a Perfect Master by millions of Indians. He and his doctrines were unknown in the West.

Shri Hans Ji Maharaj left a widow and four sons, all of whom were involved in the family religion. His precocious youngest son began preaching at the age of two and delivered his first sermon in English at age six. The father had predicted that his youngest son "would one day shine over the whole world as brightly as the sun shines in the sky." At his father's funeral, the youngster stood up and told the mourners: "Children of God, why are you weeping? . . . The Perfect Master never dies. Guru Maharaj Ji is here amongst you. Recognize him, obey him, and adore him." He, rather than one of his older brothers, assumed the leadership of the Divine Light Mission.

A few years later, thousands of Americans were looking on the pudgy teenage guru as the incarnation of God. Rennie Davis, anti-war activist and leader of the radical "Chicago Seven," was among those who have acknowledged the claims of the Maharaj Ji and joined the Divine Light Mission (DLM).

By early 1973, the DLM reported almost 500 centers around the world and about 35,000 U.S. adherents. The disappointing "Millenium '73" rally at the

Houston Astrodome and bitter feuding within the DLM's Holy Family disillusioned many young converts. A generous estimate of the cult's membership as the 1980s begin is about 8,000 in the U.S., 10,000 in Europe, another 10,000 in India, and 2,500 in Latin America.

Typically, the Indian swamis and gurus who have attempted to transplant one or another form of Hinduism to American soil have been elderly ascetics. The founders of the Hare Krishna and the Transcendental Meditation movements in the U.S. come to mind. They could hardly stand in greater contrast to the boy-guru who imported the Divine Light Mission but became known to American newspaper readers for his love of fast, expensive cars, nightclubbing, and pretty women.

Until the Maharaj Ji took over his father's role, the DLM had been confined to India, where it encountered some hostility from the more orthodox Hindu sects. In 1969, the first DLM missionary was dispatched to England. A year or so later, the guru quit the Roman Catholic mission school he had been attending and announced that he was ready to bring peace to the world. The proclamation came at the climax of a colorful parade of elephants, devotees, and camels near New Delhi. An estimated 1,500,000 people watched the spectacle.

Maharaj Ji himself flew to England in 1971 and appeared briefly at a pop-music festival; his 5-minute sermonette on this occasion was the first public exposition of DLM principles in the West. In July of the same year he arrived in the U.S. A handful of young Americans had earlier gone to India and accepted the new faith. They formed the nucleus of the U.S. branch and helped stage a rally in Colorado in 1972, which netted 2,000 converts.

The conversion of Rennie Davis stunned the counterculture and automatically brought headlines to the Maharaj Ji. Davis explained: "I'm simply doing what Guru Maharaj Ji has prepared me to do all my life. He is the Perfect Master, the creator of the world, and we are nothing but his perfect puppets."

In short order the cult expanded to embrace a record company, a magazine and newspaper, a used-clothes store, a repair shop, and a headquarters in Denver. The guru announced that the DLM would sponsor a huge rally in the Astrodome in November 1973. This three-day teach-in would be "the most important event in the history of the world." His followers spent hundreds of thousands of dollars to publicize and prepare for the great day. The Perfect Master would sit on a throne 35 feet above the floor of the auditorium surrounded by artificial waterfalls and fountains. But even though admission was free, the rally managed to attract only about 15,000 of the faithful and the curious; the Houston Astrodome had room for 50,000 more. The event did attract 24 plane-loads of devotees from other countries.

This was only the first in a series of unhappy developments that befell the cult. Until Millenium '73, the DLM had enjoyed a remarkable growth in the

U.S. To help pay debts incurred in staging the rally, the guru now asked his followers to tithe their incomes.

In May 1974 many "premies" (initiates) were shocked to hear that the 16-year-old savior had married his secretary, a former airline stewardess. She was eight years his senior. The Maharaj Ji revealed that his bride was actually the incarnation of the goddess Durga, a ten-armed, tiger-taming deity.

Then, at a public meeting, someone threw a shaving-cream pie in the guru's face, and a bodyguard-devotee fractured the culprit's skull with a blackjack. Rennie Davis told the press. "This is not the age to turn the other cheek. This Savior will not be crucified."

Trouble was stirring in the Holy Family. The Maharaj Ji's marriage, his practical jokes and adolescent behavior, his Rolls Royces, and especially his abandonment of a meatless diet scandalized his mother, who declared that the playboy guru had lost his claim to lead the DLM. The mantle would fall on his eldest brother. His mother was also miffed when she was barred from visiting the guru's $400,000 estate in Malibu. She and the older brothers took a plane back to India and began a campaign to dethrone the Maharaj Ji.

Some premies left the cult in disgust, but a dedicated core continued to revere their god-guru. A visit to an American *ashram* (DLM commune) would confirm that Maharaj Ji maintains control of the cult in the U.S. His photos cover the walls; and his cassette recordings, motion pictures, and writings form the basic instruction for novices, as well as for the initiated.

The variation of Hinduism known as the Divine Light Mission teaches that God has appeared many times in history — as Vishnu, Krishna, Buddha, Jesus Christ, and others. Each age has its Perfect Master (or Satguru). An individual's salvation lies in giving complete devotion to the current Satguru.

The cult members believe that the Maharaj Ji is God in human form and as such possesses perfect Knowledge. All human beings who pass through life without achieving enlightenment are destined to return as insects or animals. The Perfect Master is the door to Knowledge.

In Western countries, the DLM appropriates Christian terminology with its own definitions. The Maharaj Ji tells his followers that Jesus Christ was the Perfect Master for his age, but that that age is over. The DLM teachers, called mahatmas, even employ texts from the Bible to buttress the guru's claims to divinity.

The Divine Light Mission claims to offer a direct experience of God. Those who sit at the Maharaj Ji's feet can expect to see divine light, hear celestial music, and taste divine nectar.

A mahatma conducts the initiation ceremony in a darkened room decorated with pictures of the Maharaj Ji. After the lecture on DLM principles, the mahatma instructs the initiates in the secret practices of the cult. He asks each of them to press the sides of the forehead with the thumb and middle finger of the right hand, while pressing the lower center of the forehead with the index finger. If one presses hard enough, one should see "divine light." Now the mahatma sticks his fingers in the initiate's ears and induces celestial sounds. Finally, the mahatma teaches the newcomer to curl his or her tongue back into the mouth until almost swallowing it; one should then be able to taste divine nectar with the tip of one's tongue. The DLM says that Jesus lived on this divine nectar during his 40 days in the desert. (Critics say the premies simply "taste" postnasal drip.)

The fourth exercise is the most important of all. The premie is introduced to the DLM form of meditation, designed to enable one to "bliss out." The mahatma imparts a secret mantra (as in Transcendental Meditation), which forms the basis of the daily two hours of meditation.

Premies get copies of a handbook called *Life with Knowledge,* which outlines the rules for their new life. They must agree to meditate every morning and evening, attend Satsang (public lectures), surrender all possessions to the DLM, avoid swearing and attending motion pictures, and practice celibacy if unmarried. About one-tenth of the cult's members live in ashrams, but most retain their secular jobs and homes or apartments.

A former top official of the worldwide DLM, Robert Mishler, has charged that the Maharaj Ji "has bastardized the teaching of the gurus." Mishler, who left the cult in 1976, said the guru has become an object of veneration instead of a teacher of truth. "That kind of absolute dominion over people provides a corrupting influence," said the ex-DLM leader, who maintains that DLM cultists "will literally do anything he tells them."

The Maharaj Ji now has three children and he shuttles between homes in Malibu, California, and Miami, Florida, where national headquarters have been relocated. The battle in India's courts between the guru and his mother has been going on since 1975; when she broke with her son, she seized various cult assets in India — and he has sought legal remedies to get back what he says is his property.

For a few years, in the early 1970s, the Divine Light Mission seemed on the verge of becoming one of the major cults on the American scene. The troubles surrounding the overblown Houston rally, the guru's teen-age marriage, and the defection of the rest of his family have seriously eroded membership rolls and support.

Astrology as a Cult

Most of the cults discussed in this book demand the primary religious loyalty of their adherents. No one can logically be a Methodist and a Moonie at the same time, or a Baptist and a Hare Krishna devotee. Astrology displays some of the characteristics of a cult but does not demand this exclusive loyalty. Millions of Protestant and Catholic believers have some degree of fascination with astrology; but only a few people seek a comprehensive religious orientation from the stars. For such people, astrology is indeed a religious cult.

For thousands of years, human beings have looked at the night skies and speculated that perhaps the stars had some influence on their lives and on the fortunes of their communities. Systematic speculation of that kind, known as astrology, fell into disrepute in the 18th century. Now, in our age, when humans have actually walked on the moon and sent satellites into space in order to take close-up photographs of Saturn, astrology has staged an amazing revival.

Millions of Americans govern their daily activities according to the "advice" of their horoscopes; and many more satisfy their curiosity by checking an astrology column in their newspaper. Out of 1,750 daily newspapers in this country, more than 1,200 carry a regular astrology column. A recent Gallup poll indicates that 29 percent of Americans believe in astrology; 10 percent in witches, 11 percent in ghosts, and 57 percent in UFOs. Another survey reports that more than half the populations of England, France, and West Germany also consult horoscopes.

There are an estimated 10,000 professional astrologists in the U.S. Business has never been better for them and their 150,000 colleagues who practice the "astral art" in their spare time. Many professional astrologers list their office hours in the Yellow Pages of telephone books; their fee ranges from $25 to $300 for preparing a person's horoscope. They can affiliate with a national professional organization, study astrology in several schools, and brush up on their skills at numerous seminars and conferences.

At least twenty magazines devoted to astrology are currently being published. The devotee can buy a wide assortment of books explaining how to cook by astrology, find a mate with compatible constellations, or invest successfully in the stock market with the help of the stars.

Even the computer has been put to use by the astrologers. One firm provides a 10,000-word horoscope for $20; date, time, and place of birth are fed into an IBM 360-40 computer. Another company mails personalized horoscopes, prepared by computer, every three months, and bills clients $9 for each one.

The hit musical *Hair* has popularized the common astrological belief that humankind has now entered the Age of Aquarius. The Piscean age of sorrow and trouble ended in 1904, and, astrologically speaking, we can now look forward to 2,000 years of peace and brotherhood. World Wars I and II did not get the Age of Aquarius off to a promising start, but true believers are sure the world has begun a new and promising cycle.

Astrology is actually one manifestation of a new interest in the occult. Readers devour the prophecies of "seers," such as Jeane Dixon and the late Edgar Cayce. Such relics of a prescientific age as numerology, Tarot cards, witchcraft, palmistry, and phrenology, as well as astrology, have suddenly become objects of serious study by housewives, college students, professional men, writers, and artists.

In a complex and often bewildering world, astrology promises some answers and some guidance for millions of people. Worldwide, it probably claims more adherents than it has had at any time during the past 200 years. Some observers attribute its popularity to a general turn toward anti-scientism: a sense that the wonders of science have brought about not only material progress but also wars, pollution, and a general sense of frustration. Others see astrology and the occult occupying ground once held by institutional religion.

Although astrology held an honored place in Babylonian, Greek, and Roman societies, it was discredited by the rise of science and new knowledge. In 1960, only a few enthusiasts continued to believe that the position of the sun, moon, and planets at the moment of an individual's birth exercised a powerful influence on his or her character or life-history.

For several millenia, such ancient peoples as the Chaldeans, Egyptians, Assyrians, Hindus, Babylonians, and Chinese studied the movements and relative positions of stars and planets; they devised horoscopic systems by means of which human character could be analyzed and future events foretold. The Babylonians undoubtedly made the greatest contribution to systematization of astrology. Astrological charts found on clay tablets near ancient Babylon date from 3,000 B.C.

Babylonian priests identified four planets (now known as Mercury, Venus, Mars, and Jupiter). They kept careful records of the movements of these bodies, as well as of the sun and moon. They lacked telescopes. But from towers built on flat lands, they could scan the complete horizon.

At first the Babylonian priests taught that the planets themselves were gods; but later they came to believe that a god ruled each planet. As they elaborated their ideas, they associated each planet with certain characteristics. Sometimes the apparent color of a planet gave them a clue: "reddish" Mars was identified with war and bloodshed.

From observation of the planets, and aided by a lively imagination and a keen desire to make them intelligible, the ancients developed a complex lore that attributed meaning (and purpose) to the various positions of the heavenly bodies. At first their predictions concerned only the fate of nations; but eventually horoscopes were drawn for individuals. The first such personal horoscope we know of was made about 263 B.C.

From Babylon, astrology was carried to Greece, where further developments took place. The Greeks reasoned that if the sun and moon had such obvious influences on the tides and temperatures, the other planets might well determine aspects of human life. Plato and Aristotle both believed that the stars were divine. Hippocrates declared: "The man who does not understand astrology is to be called fool rather than physician." (Despite the contemporary revival of astrology, the subject has not been reintroduced into the medical-school curriculum.)

Greek slaves brought astrology to Rome during the Punic Wars (3rd-2nd cent. B.C.). Before long, almost all the Romans took it for granted that the stars had a major influence on persons and events. Early Latin scientific writers, such as Pliny and Seneca, offered some mild criticism of astrology; but both assumed the validity of its basic principles.

Christianity alternated between toleration of, and bitter opposition to, astrology. St. Augustine attacked astrology on the basis that it negated man's free will. He used the argument of the diversity in the life-history of twins as conclusive evidence that astrology was either hokum or the work of demons. "The astrologers say: 'It is from the heavens that the irresistible cause of sin comes, it is due to the conjunction of Venus with Mars or Saturn.' Thus man is absolved of all faults, he who is only proudly rotting flesh. The blame is indeed given to the creator and ruler of the heavens and of the stars."

Other early Christian opponents of astrology include St. Basil, St. Gregory of Nyssa, St. John Chrysostom, and St. Ambrose. "As part of paganism, the practice of all divinatory arts was forbidden the Christian; and, in the writings of the earlier apologists, astrology is hardly differentiated from soothsaying, oracles, and magic. In its philosophical dress, astrology was even less acceptable. The fatalism implied in the belief that the stars are arbiters of human destinies never found more unyielding opponents than the Church Fathers" (T.O. Wedel, *The Medieval Attitude toward Astrology,* repr. Archon Books 1968, pp. 15-16).

Astrologers tried to defend their "science" in an increasingly Christian culture during the Middle Ages in the West, by pointing out the role of their "colleagues," the Magi, in the Christmas story. Christian apologists retorted that the Magi renounced their belief in astrology at the cradle in Bethlehem and, significantly, returned home by a different route.

The revival of Aristotelian and Arabian learning in the 12th century gave a boost to astrology. The Arabs had developed not only mathematics and medicine far beyond European levels, but had paid considerable attention to the perfection of astrological knowledge.

St. Thomas Aquinas, in the 13th century, formulated a compromise that allowed astrologers and Churchmen to live in peace. The Angelic Doctor admitted that stars influence the body, and that the body in turn influences the intellect and will: "The majority of men, in fact, are governed by their passions, which are dependent upon bodily appetites; in these the influence of the stars is clearly felt. Few indeed are the wise who are capable of resisting their animal instincts. Astrologers, consequently, are able to foretell the truth in the majority of cases, especially when they undertake general predictions" (*Summa* i.i. 115).

The astrologers, for their part, eager to placate the Church, generally left a place for free will in their system. They argued that the stars exerted an influence on all people, but that they could resist those influences. For example, a horoscope might reveal that a person has a strong tendency toward selfishness. Knowing this, the selfishly-inclined person can make an extra effort to cultivate generosity.

Fr. Kenneth J. Delano, an astronomer and severe critic of astrology, comments: "The medieval Christians were able to pacify their consciences as regards astrology by disclaiming any belief in the pagan religions to which astrology owes its origin. Furthermore, most Christians who accepted astrology were cautious enough to insist that the stars only indicate probabilities or tendencies, thus leaving room for man's free will and God's intervening graces" *(Astrology: Fact or Fiction?,* p. 44).

Throughout the Middle Ages, most people believed that the stars did influence human life. Astrology was taught at several leading universities between 1200 and 1600. Pope Julius II (d. 1513) set the date for his coronation by astrology; and Pope Paul III (d. 1549) consulted his astrologers before setting the date for any Church consistory. Pope Leo X (d. 1521) founded a chair of astrology at the Sapienza. So long as astrology ruled out fatalism and made some room for free will, it coexisted with the medieval Church.

Astrology held its own until the middle of the 18th century. By then the advances in astronomy and the re-orientation of thought demanded by new developments in science had shaken the older worldview of astrology. Since 1781, and the invention of the telescope, additional planets have been discovered: Uranus, Neptune, Pluto. Even unsophisticated people questioned the value of astrological calculations based on the wrong number of planets. Chairs of astrology in the European universities disappeared, as its study as a genuine science was discredited.

Until recent years, astrology was derided, and people found it hard to believe that earlier scientists had ever swallowed the myths and assumptions of astrology. Historians of science honored astrologers as the precursors of astronomy, as they acknowledged the debt of the chemists to the alchemists; but they gave no credence to astrological analysis. Even though popes and theologians had once pinned their faith on astrology, the Catholic Church again began to condemn all astrology as a form of divination.

Perhaps the one person most responsible for renewing interest in astrology in the United States was a Boston astrologer, Evangeline Adams (d. 1932). She polished her reputation by casting horoscopes for such famous personalities as financier J. P. Morgan, singer Enrico Caruso, and actress Mary Pickford. Through her efforts, the courts removed astrology from the category of fortune-telling, which was widely regarded by law as a criminal offense.

Miss Adams explained: "It should be clearly understood that the stars only indicate what will come to pass if intelligence and free will are not used to change the natural course of events. The wise man cooperates with the stars, the fool thinks he rules them." She reaffirmed the old astrological saying: "The stars impel, they do not compel." People can assert themselves against the influence of the stars, just as they can fight hereditary or environmental factors in their lives.

At the time of her death, Evangeline Adams had been conducting a popular radio program on astrology and was receiving 4,000 requests a week for horoscopes and personal advice. One of her converts, Carroll Righter, has become the best known astrologer in the U.S.

Righter attended the University of Pennsylvania and later received a law degree. Of independent means, he engaged in various philanthropic activities during the Depression and started to investigate astrology in order to disprove its claims. Instead he became an enthusiast, and emerged as a professional astrologer in 1939. In 1980, his syndicated column was being carried by more than 300 newspapers, with a total circulation of some 30 million.

Nobody would dispute the all-purpose advice Righter offers in his column. For example, on June 15, 1979, he advised those born under the sign of Aries to "consult an expert for the advice you need." Capricorns were told, "Be more cheerful." For Pisces it was "Steer clear of one who has an eye on your assets." Libras were told, "Handle your money wisely."

Some of his faithful clients in Hollywood have been Robert Cummings, Tyrone Power, Van Johnson, Marlene Dietrich, Peter Lawford, and Ronald Reagan. Many stars refuse to make any decision regarding their careers or love life without consulting their favorite astrologer. Jackie Gleason was once told by an astrologer that he would risk death if he took a plane; he has not traveled by plane since. A prominent young actress was asked by an interviewer why she had not married. She solemnly replied: "To me marriage is a sacred state and as a Catholic I would never enter marriage unless I was sure it would last a lifetime. . . . Besides, my astrologer told me not to marry before I was thirty." One well known psychic, Jeane Dixon, relates that she learned astrology from a Jesuit priest at Loyola University in Los Angeles.

During World War II, the allies knew that Hitler retained a court astrologer and probably made some of his military decisions on the basis of the stars. The British hired Louis de Wohl, an astrologer, author, and Catholic, to cast Hitler's horoscope and try to guess what the German astrologers were telling the Führer. Regardless of nationality or politics, any professional astrologer should reach about the same conclusions and offer about the same advice for a given set of birth data. Despite Hitler's patronage, German astrologers fell on hard times after the flight of Rudolf Hess to England. Hess too retained a personal astrologer and was believed to be under his spell.

The present widespread interest in astrology in the United States and Canada is a recent phenomenon. In many parts of the world, belief in astrology is taken for granted by almost all people. In India, Pakistan, Ceylon, and Burma, practically everyone checks with an astrologer about a proposed marriage, about the propitious date for an undertaking, or about business deals. An East Indian astrologer must study for 20 years before he is given a government license for public practice.

To gain more insight into the work of an astrologer, I asked a professional to prepare my horoscope. Mrs. Frederick Geiger, who had been practicing astrology for 20 years, belonged to the American Federation of Astrologers.

Besides astrological consultations and preparing horoscopes (sometimes for popular figures such as Bill Cosby and Phyllis Diller), Mrs. Geiger has taught a class in astrology for about fifty Purdue University students enrolled in the so-called Free University. She insists that astrology rests on a firm scientific basis, but offers no explanation of how planets actually affect human lives.

Like all astrologers, Mrs. Geiger works from basic information: the day, hour, and place of birth. She must adjust the birth-hour to account for such complications as daylight-saving time. To the conscientious practitioner, the difference of even an hour can distort a horoscope. Using a book of ephemeris (a table of planetary positions) and computing the correct astral time, the astrologer begins to construct the horoscope. This is a sort of map showing the position of the sun, moon, and planets in relation to the earth, and the signs of the Zodiac, at the moment of the client's birth.

The ancients devised the system of the twelve signs of the Zodiac, which correspond to about thirty days on the calendar. The location of the sun in a particular sign is considered of prime importance. This sun-sign determines whether a person is an Aries, Taurus, Gemini, Cancer (Moonchild), Leo, Virgo, Libra, Scorpio, Sagittarius, Capricorn, Aquarius, or Pisces. Another important factor is the sign that is ascending (or rising) at the moment of a client's birth. In my case, I was found to be a Capricorn (my birthday is January 1, and Capricorn includes those born between December 22 and January 19), with Sagittarius rising.

Capricorns, I was told, are thoughtful, serious, somewhat ambitious, economical, hard-working. They are blessed with good reasoning ability and make the most of opportunities. With Sagittarius ascending, Mrs. Geiger told me, I was also inclined to be jovial, bright, hopeful, generous, and charitable. My disposition was likely to be frank, fearless, impulsive, demonstrative, outspoken, nervously energetic, sincere, and quick to arrive at conclusions.

Although the position of the sun and the ascending sign are of special importance, the positions of the other planets are significant, too. The locations of these planets in various "houses" and their relationships to one another are studied. (Like other professions, astrology revels in its own jargon — such as "cusps," "aspects," "houses," and "triplicities.")

Mrs. Geiger loaned me one of the standard texts used by those who prepare horoscopes: *A to Z Horoscope Maker and Delineator*, by Llewellyn George. The author of this 812-page-volume promoted the study of "scientific," as opposed to occult, astrology. He saw a bright future for the art: "It is only a question of time when the United States and other nations will find astrology indispensable for an orderly arrangement and conduct of affairs in harmony with natural laws."

Most of the characteristics in anyone's horoscope will be traits people like to hear about. One would have to come up with an unusual combination of planetary influences to produce a horoscope indicating that a person was ornery, stingy, self-centered, and ugly.

Llewellyn George's book describes the particular influence of each heavenly body. We are told that the moon governs the brain, stomach, and breasts, the left eye of the male, and the right eye of the female. This information has probably not changed since it was first inferred by the Babylonian wise men a few thousands years ago. It means as much today as it meant then.

Mrs. Geiger offered no explanation of how or why the positions of the planets at the moment I drew my first breath, in Michigan City, Indiana, should exert a force in my life. She did maintain that she had never drawn up a horoscope that did not accurately reflect the personality of the client.

Some astrologers do advance theories of astrological causality. George attributes the influence to "magnetic currents" set in motion at the time of birth. Someone might ask why other variables do not produce a similar influence. These variables might include the prevailing winds, pollen count, temperature, Dow Jones average, or barometer reading. Another astrologer, in a tentative explanation, points out that the moon causes the ebb and flow of tides; and as the human body is 70 percent water, it too may be affected by the moon. But astronomer Bart J. Bok points out: "If we are to believe that the influence of a mere mass of matter affects human character, then certainly the Empire State Building would have vastly more effect on people in New York than would a planet millions of miles away."

Perhaps most astrologers who offer any rationale fall back on the theory of the accumulated wisdom of the ages. They say if you take 1,000 people and discover that most tall people were born in July, and most short people in December, and if you continue such an analysis for 50 centuries or so, you will build up the kind of lore on which the astrologers draw.

Most scientists and intellectuals scorn astrology. You cannot take an astrology course at the more prestigious universities in the U.S. One of the few respected scholars in recent times to show any interest in astrology was the psychologist Carl Jung. He often arranged to have horoscopes drawn up for his patients and was impressed by what they revealed. Jung urged closer examination of the claims of astrology, and commented: "Today, rising out of the social deeps, astrology knocks at the doors of the universities, from which it was banished some 300 years ago." Jung is also reported to have said: "We are born at a given moment, in a given place and, like vintage years of wine, we have the qualities of the year and of the season in which we are born. Astrology does not lay claim to anything more."

Critics of astrology say that published horoscopes are so general they can apply to almost anyone; and that astrologers boast about their (rare) bull's-eyes but keep silent about the (more numerous) misses. Serious astrologers look upon the kind of astrology presented in the columns of daily newspapers as practically useless. These columns classify people only by the sun-sign, which is "important" but accounts for only about 25 percent of the influences charted by professional astrologers.

The outlandish language and outdated concepts of contemporary astrology turn sophisticated people away. They know that planets do not "rise" in the night sky; instead the earth "turns toward" the planet. Astrologers talk about the "conjunction" of planets; but at such moments the conjunct planets are still actually millions of miles apart. Finally, except for the light and heat of the sun and the effect on the tides by the moon, the changes in light, gravitation, and magnetism produced by the other planets are so slight they can hardly affect human character. Someone might allow for the possibility of some influence by the moon, which is next door to earth, on the human body, but hesitate to admit any such influence by Jupiter, which is 390,000,000 miles away when it is closest to earth.

The live-and-let-live compromise between the Catholic Church and astrology lasted for several centuries after Aquinas; but more recently the Church has returned to a general attitude of condemnation. The Church discourages dabbling in astrology and the occult. Eager to protect the concept of free will, most Christian moralists have agreed with the words of Cassius in Shakespeare's *Julius Caesar:*

> The fault, dear Brutus, lies not in our Stars
> But in ourselves that we are underlings.

The Vatican magazine *Osservatore della Domenica* carried an article about astrology in 1961, written by Father Reginaldo Francisco. He stated: "If one really believes in the horoscope one commits a grave sin. One falls into heresy by denying free will and one violates the first commandment." Oddly enough, the popular women's magazine *Cosi,* published by Italian nuns, has featured an astrology column on a regular basis for years.

A 1940 statement by the American Society for Psychological Research dismissed astrology as nonsense: "There is no evidence that astrology has any value whatever in revealing the past, the present, or the future fate of any human being, and there is not the slightest reason for believing that social events can be predicted by astrology." A Dominican priest and student of the occult, Father Richard Woods, takes a somewhat different view: "By implication, there may well be a basis for astrological claims if for no other purpose than as a psychological shorthand by which we can describe character traits based on planetary configurations. At any rate, based on thousands of years of observation, there does seem to be an uncanny correspondence between traditional astrological interpretations of character based on the sun-sign as modified by the positions of the moon and planets" (*The Occult Revolution*, p. 92).

Uncanny correspondence or not, Father Delano concludes that no Christian should get involved in the study of astrology, even for amusement. "When a person accepts astrology, he acts in violation of common sense, good reason, empirical science, and religion. Science and reason alone offer enough objections to dissuade any sensible person from believing in astrology, but religion presents additional arguments to show why people are obliged by God not to put faith in astrology" (p. 106). He adds: "Christians are obliged to shun astrology not only because it is pagan in origin and in its basic philosophy, but also because of its latent determinism, overt hedonism, and disgraceful irrationalism, all of which are unbecoming of God's faithful" (p. 126).

Nearly 200 prominent scientists in such fields as astronomy, psychology, biology, and statistics signed a statement in 1976 branding astrologers as charlatans and declaring it is "simply a mistake to imagine that the forces exerted by stars and planets at the moment of birth can shape our future." Prof. Paul Hurtz of the philosophy department of the State University of New York at Buffalo served as chairman of the committee. He stated: "Thus far we have not found any conclusive test establishing the validity of classic, popular astrology." He added, "Even astrologers grant that sun sign astrology is totally inaccurate and insufficient as a prediction of personality or types of future behavior."

Some people claim to be able to analyze character by studying handwriting, or by examining the bumps on a person's head, or by matching color preferences with personality traits. The scientific foundation for these methods is not much sounder than for astrology, but the Church has never formally called such practices into question. The average Christian American who takes an interest in astrology is not rejecting free will or falling into heresy. His or her attitude is one of curiosity. People might be exhorted to spend their time more wisely, but so might the enthusiasts who devote what may seem excessive time to other enthusiasms commonly met with in U.S. culture, whether it be golf, professional football contests, bridge, or bingo.

Perhaps the wisest course for the Church is still that suggested by St. Thomas Aquinas. If a Christian accepts a theory of astrology that denies free will and puts humans at the mercy of the stars, such a person thereby rejects his or her religious faith. If one simply thinks — with or without much scientific confirmation — that the position of the stars at the moment of one's birth has or may have an influence on one's personality and fortunes, one may be self-deluded — but one does not thereby contradict any specific Christian doctrine. Self-delusion is one way in which one can diminish one's humanity, however, as St. Thomas also held.

Condemning astrology as a form of divination is largely beside the point, because hardly any Western astrologers believe that God (or gods) inhabit or direct the planets; unless divinity is involved, no divination is possible, even in theory.

Personally I do not put much stock in astrology, and do not see why the position of, say, Saturn at 2 a.m. on January 1, 1926, has anything to do with my health, stock-market luck, or love life. But if anyone wants to suppose that he or she can help explain my character by calculating the position of the planets, I'm inclined to be tolerant — perhaps because I am a Capricorn, with Sagittarius ascending, and am therefore inclined to be "jovial, bright, hopeful, generous, and charitable."

Sources of Further Information

Braden, Charles S., *These Also Believe* (New York: Macmillan, 1949). A classic study of cults and minority religions by a professor of the history and literature of religions. Braden examines such minority groups as Christian Science and Mormonism, as well as some groups that have practically disappeared in the intervening three decades since publication, such as Psychiana, I Am, The Oxford Group, and Father Divine's Peace Mission. Objective and scholarly.

Breese, David, *Know the Marks of Cults* (Wheaton, Ill.: Victor Books, 1975). A survey of old and new cults by an evangelical Protestant writer. Describes a dozen characteristics that all cults share, including "presumptuous messianic leadership," financial exploitation, defective Christology, and an enslaving organizational structure.

Clements, R. D., *God and the Gurus* (Downers Grove, Ill.: Inter-Varsity Press, 1975). The author, who holds a doctorate from the Imperial College in London, limits his consideration to the general characteristics of Eastern religions imported to the United States and devotes chapters to the Hare Krishna movement, the Divine Light Mission, and Transcendental Meditation.

Conway, Flo, and Jim Siegelman, *Snapping: America's Epidemic of Sudden Personality Change* (Philadelphia: Lippincott, 1978). Through numerous case studies, the authors examine the sudden personality changes that many young people undergo when they affiliate with such cults as the Church of Scientology and the Unification Church.

Ellwood, Robert S., *Alternative Altars* (Univ. of Chicago Press, 1979). The author studies three religious movements outside the mainstream of Judeo-Christian life in this country: Spiritualism, Theosophy, and American Zen. *Religious and Spiritual Groups in Modern America* (Englewood Cliffs, N.J.: Prentice-Hall, 1973). A major contribution to the understanding of cults and other minority religious groups by a professor of religion. Brief descriptions of dozens of such groups are followed by exerpts from their scriptures or from the writings of their founder-prophets.

Enroth, Ronald, *Brainwashing and the Extremist Cults* (Grand Rapids: Zondervan, 1977). *The Lure of the Cults* (Chappaqua, N.Y.: Christian Herald Books, 1979). This sociologist-author examines five categories of new religious movements: Eastern mystical; aberrational Christian; psycho-spiritual or self-improvement; eclectic-syncretistic; and psychic-occult-astral groups. Includes advice for parents whose children have been attracted by contemporary cults.

Helfy, James C., *The Youth Nappers* (Wheaton, Ill.: Victor Books, 1977). A popular treatment of some two-dozen cults from a conservative Protestant perspective, with the aim of refuting their beliefs. The writer says he will help the reader to understand "what you can do to prevent the spread of the demonic virus of modern cults."

MacCollam, Joel A., *Carnival of Souls* (New York: Seabury, 1979). An Episcopal priest, who is also a consultant to his church on the cult phenomenon, examines the cults' appeal to young people, the reaction of parents, deprogramming, testimonies of ex-members, and so forth.

Martin, Walter, *The Kingdom of the Cults* (Grand Rapids: Zondervan, 1965). A reference work on the older cults written from a conservative Protestant stance. More concerned with such movements as Mormonism, Christian Science, Spiritualism, and the like, than with the cults that have gained prominence since the book was written. The author's definition of a cult embraces Unitarianism.

Melton, J. Gordon, *Encyclopedia of American Religions,* 2 vols. (Wilmington, N.C.: Consortium, 1980). Monumental reference work on 1,200 churches, sects, and cults in the United States compiled by a Methodist minister and student of comparative religion. Volume 2 describes scores of little-known cults, as well as almost all of those that regularly make headlines. A major contribution to the field.

Needleman, Jacob, and George Baker, eds., *Understanding the New Religions* (New York: Seabury, 1978). Prominent scholars of comparative religion contributed papers to a conference on the study of new religious movements, sponsored by the Graduate Theological Union at Berkeley, in 1977. Most of those papers are reprinted here.

Needleman, Jacob, *The New Religions* (New York: Doubleday, 1970).

Patrick, Ted, *Let My Children Go* (New York: Dutton, 1976). A well known deprogrammer offers his apologia for abducting and deprogramming members of a number of cults. The author claims to have supervised about 7,000 such deprogrammings.

Petersen, William J., *Those Curious New Cults* (New Canaan, Conn.: Keats, 1975), The editor of *Eternity* magazine devotes chapters to 18 contemporary cults. Besides most of the better-known movements, he looks at Meher Baba, I Ching, Gurdjieff, and Satanism. He enumerates nine spiritual, psychological, and sociological reasons why people are attracted by the cults.

Randi, James, *Flim-Flam* (New York: Lippincott & Crowell, 1980). The author attempts to debunk astrology, Transcendental Meditation, Scientology, Edgar Cayce, spiritualism, UFOs, and the paranormal in general.

Rowley, Peter, *New Gods in America* (New York: David McKay, 1971).

Rudin, James and Marcia, *Prison or Paradise? The New Religious Cults* (Philadelphia: Fortress, 1980). The authors examine nine major cults and their appeal to white, middle-class collegians. They offer guidelines for parents, describe deprogramming techniques, and provide a list of counter-cult organizations.

Sparks, Jack, *The Mind Benders* (Nashville, Tenn.: Thomas Nelson, 1977). Breezy descriptions of the history, beliefs, and methods of three Hindu and four "Christian" cults, accompanied by refutations of their doctrines by appeal to biblical texts.

Stewart, Louis, *Life Forces: A Contemporary Guide to the Cult and Occult* (Kansas City, Mo: Andrews and McMeel, 1980). The author demonstrates an encyclopedic knowledge of scores of occult groups, from ancient times to the present. His accounts are enlivened by a touch of humor and a healthy skepticism of some aspects of occult lore. His wry and detailed instructions on how to fake a spiritualist seance if one's psychic powers are weakening are especially enlightening.

Storer, Carroll, and Jo Anne Parker, *All God's Children: The Cult Experience — Salvation of Slavery?* (Radnor, Pa.: Chilton, 1977). Two journalists interviewed dozens of cultists and former members of such groups as the Moonies, Hare Krishnas, and Children of God. These case histories and the authors' interpretations offer useful insights into the workings of these movements.

Streiker, Lowell D., *The Cults Are Coming!* (Nashville, Tenn.: Abingdon, 1978). The executive director of a mental-health association, with a doctorate in religion from Princeton, devotes most of his discussion to the Hare Krishnas, Moonies, and Children of God. Despite its rather sensational title, this is one of the more scholarly and solid contributions to the literature about the cults.

Verdier, Paul A., *Brainwashing and the Cults* (North Hollywood, Calif.: Wilshire, 1977). A clinical psychologist maintains that a number of cults employ brainwashing techniques and hypnosis to win converts and retain their loyalty. These methods include isolation, endless lectures, fatigue, peer pressure, low protein diet, mantras, the repetition of meaningless sounds, and chanting.

Whalen, William J., *Minority Religions in America,* rev. ed. (Staten Island, N.Y.: Alba House, 1981). While all cults are minority religions, not all minority religions are cults. This book describes such bodies as the Mennonites, Salvation Army, Quakers, Baha'is, Hutterites, Rosicrucians, Swedenborgians, and Theosophists. *Separated Brethren,* rev. ed. (Huntington, Ind.: Our Sunday Visitor, 1979). Written as an introduction to the major Protestant denominations for Catholic readers, this book also includes brief treatments of such cults as the Moonies and Hare Krishnas.

Woods, Richard, *The Occult Revolution* (New York: Herder, 1971). A Dominican priest examines the revival of interest in the occult, which he attributes to a religious response to the impact of technological change. He looks at astrology, witchcraft, Satanism, and other manifestations of the occult.

Zaretsky, Irving I., and Mark P. Leone, eds., *Religious Movements in Contemporary America* (Princeton Univ. Press, 1974). An 837-page study of numerous marginal religious movements in the U.S. by a group of scholars. Of special interest are sections on Scientology, Jehovah's Witnesses, witchcraft, Mormonism, and Hare Krishna.

WITCHCRAFT

Adler, Margot, *Drawing Down the Moon* (New York: Viking, 1979).

Gardner, Gerald, *Witchcraft Today* (New York: Citadel, 1970).

Holzer, Hans, *Pagans and Witches* (New York: Manor, 1978).

LaVey, Anton, *The Satanic Bible* (New York: Avon, 1969).

Roberts, Susan, *Witches, U.S.A.* (New York: Dell, 1970).

Schurmacher, Emile, *Witchcraft in America Today* (New York: Paperback Library, 1970).

Seth, Ronald, *Witches and Their Craft* (New York: Taplinger, 1968).

Tindall, Gillian, *Handbook on Witches* (New York: Atheneum, 1966).
Valienta, Doreen, *Witchcraft for Tomorrow* (New York: St. Martin's, 1978).

JEHOVAH'S WITNESSES

Beckford, James A., *The Trumpet of Prophecy* (Oxford: Basil Blackwell, 1975).
Gruss, Edmond Charles, *Apostles of Denial* (Nutley, N.J.: Presbyterian and Reformed Publishing Co., 1970).
Harrison, Barbara Grizzuti, *Visions of Glory: A History and Memory of Jehovah's Witnesses* (New York: Simon & Schuster, 1978).
Stevenson, W. C., *The Inside Story of Jehovah's Witnesses* (New York: Hart, 1967).
Whalen, William J., *Armageddon Around the Corner: A Report on Jehovah's Witnesses* (New York: John Day, 1962).

SELF-REALIZATION FELLOWSHIP

Paramahansa Yoganda, *Autobiography of a Yogi* (Los Angeles: Self-Realization Fellowship, 1946).
Thomas, Wendell, *Hinduism Invades America* (New York: Beacon, 1930).

WORLDWIDE CHURCH OF GOD

Campbell, Roger F., *Herbert W. Armstrong and His Worldwide Church of God* (Fort Washington, Pa.: Christian Literature Crusade, 1974).
Chambers, Roger R., *The Plain Truth about Armstrongism* (Grand Rapids: Baker, 1972).
Hopkins, Joseph, *The Armstrong Empire* (Grand Rapids: Eerdmans, 1974).
Rader, Stanley R., *Against the Gates of Hell* (New York: Everest House, 1980).

EDGAR CAYCE AND THE A.R.E.

Cayce, Hugh Lynn, *Venture Inward* (New York: Harper & Row, 1964).
Cerminara, Gina, *Many Mansions* (New York: New American Library, 1967).
Millard, Joseph, *Edgar Cayce: Mystery Man of Miracles* (Virginia Beach: Edgar Cayce Foundation, 1967).
Sharma, I. C., *Cayce, Karma, and Reincarnation* (New York: Harper & Row, 1975).
Stern, Jess, *Edgar Cayce: The Sleeping Prophet* (Garden City, N.Y.: Doubleday, 1967).
Sugrue, Thomas, *There Is a River* (New York: Holt, Rinehart & Winston, 1942).

MOONIES

Bjornstad, James, *The Moon Is Not the Son* (Minneapolis: Dimension, 1976).

Boettcher, Robert, with Gordon L. Freedman, *Gifts of Deceit: Sun Myung Moon, Tongsun Park, and the Korean Scandal* (New York: Holt, Rinehart & Winston, 1980).

Bryant, M.D., and H. W. Richardson, eds., *A Time for Consideration: A Scholarly Appraisal of the Unification Church* (New York: Edwin Mellen Press, 1978).

Divine Principle (Washington, D.C.: The Holy Spirit Association for the Unification of World Christianity, 1973).

Edwards, Christopher, *Crazy for God* (Englewood Cliffs, N.J.: Prentice-Hall, 1979).

Horowitz, Irving Louis, ed., *Science, Sin, and Scholarship: The Politics of Reverend Moon and the Unification Church* (M.I.T. Press, 1978).

Jones, W. Farley, ed., *A Prophet Speaks Today: The Words of Sun Myung Moon* (New York: HSA-UWC Publications, 1975).

Kim, Young Oon, *Unification Theology and Christian Thought* (New York: Golden Gate, 1975).

Sontag, Frederick, *Sun Myung Moon and the Unification Church* (Nashville, Tenn.: Abingdon, 1977).

Underwood, Barbara, and Betty Underwood, *Hostage to Heaven* (New York: Clarkson Potter, 1979).

Wood, Allen Tate, with Jack Vitek, *Moonstruck: Memoirs of My Life in a Cult* (New York: Morrow, 1979).

Yamamoto, J. Isamu, *The Puppet Master* (Downers Grove, Ill.: Inter-Varsity Press, 1977).

SCIENTOLOGY

Copper, Paulette, *The Scandal of Scientology* (New York: Tower, 1971).

Garrison, Omar V., *Playing Dirty: The Secret War Against Beliefs* (Los Angeles: Ralston-Pilot, 1980).

Hubbard, L. Ron, *Dianetics: The Modern Science of Mental Health* (New York: Hermitage House, 1950).

Meldal-Johnsen, T., and P. Lusey, *The Truth about Scientology* (New York: Grosset & Dunlap, 1980).

Wallis, Roy, *The Road to Total Freedom: A Sociological Analysis of Scientology* (Columbia University Press, 1977).

What Is Scientology? (Los Angeles: Church of Scientology of California, 1978).

TRANSCENDENTAL MEDITATION

Benson, Herbert, *The Relaxation Response* (New York: Morrow, 1975).

Ebon, Martin, *Maharishi the Guru* (New York: New American Library, 1968).

Helleberg, Marilyn M., *Beyond TM: A Practical Guide to the Lost Traditions of Christian Meditation* (New York: Paulist, 1981).

Maharishi Mahesh Yogi, *The Science of Being and Art of Living* (London: George Allen and Unwin, 1963).

Robbins, Jhan, and David Fisher, *Tranquility without Pills: All about Transcendental Meditation* (New York: Bantam, 1972).

HARE KRISHNA

Daner, Francine Jeanne, *The American Children of Krsna* (New York: Holt, Rinehart and Winston, 1976).

Harper, Marvin Henry, *Gurus, Swamis, and Avatars* (Philadelphia: Westminster Press, 1972).

Judah, J. Stillson, *Hare Krishna and the Counterculture* (New York: Wiley, 1974).

Levine, Faye, *The Strange World of the Hare Krishnas* (New York: Fawcett, 1974).

Prabupada, Swami, *Bhagavad-Gita As It Is* (Los Angeles: Bhaktivedanta Book Trust, 1971).

CHILDREN OF GOD

Enroth, Ronald M., Edward E. Ericson, and C. P. Peters, *The Jesus People* (Grand Rapids: Eerdmans, 1972).

THE WAY

MacCollam, Joel A., *The Way of Victor Paul Wierwille* (Downers Grove, Ill.: Inter-Varsity Press, 1978).

Wallenstedt, Alan, *The Way: A Biblical Analysis* (Berkeley, Calif.: Spiritual Counterfeits Project, 1976).

Wierwille, Victor Paul, *Power for Abundant Living* (New Knoxville, Ohio: American Christian Press, 1971).

———, *Jesus Christ Is Not God* (New Knoxville, Ohio: American Christian Press, 1975).

Williams, J. L., *Victor Paul Wierwille and The Way International* (Chicago: Moody Press, 1979).

DIVINE LIGHT MISSION

Cameron, Charles, ed., *Who Is the Guru Maharaj Ji?* (New York: Bantam, 1973).

ASTROLOGY

Delano, Kenneth J., *Astrology: Fact or Fiction?* (Huntington, Ind.: Our Sunday Visitor, 1973).

Hone, Margaret E., *The Modern Textbook of Astrology*, 4th ed. (London: Fowler, 1968).

Howe, Ellic, *Urania's Children: The Strange World of the Astrologers* (London: Kimber, 1967).

Jones, Marc Edmund, *Astrology: How and Why It Works* (New York: Penguin, 1971).

McIntosh, Christopher, *The Astrologers and Their Creed* (London: Hutchinson, 1969).

Sakoian, Frances, and Louis S. Acker, *The Astrologer's Handbook* (New York: Harper & Row, 1973).

Index